C000143198

# KNOTS AND ROPEWORK

## Nola Trower

**Helmsman Books**

First published in 1992 by
Helmsman Books, an imprint of
The Crowood Press Ltd
Ramsbury, Marlborough
Wiltshire SN8 2HR

© The Crowood Press Ltd 1992

All rights reserved. No part of this publication may be reproduced or transmitted in any form or by any means, electronic or mechanical, including photocopy, recording, or any information storage and retrieval system, without permission in writing from the publishers.

**British Library Cataloguing in Publication Data**

A catalogue record for this book is available from the British Library

ISBN 1 85223 705 8

**Picture credits**
All photographs and line-drawings by Nola Trower

**Dedication**
To Spike, whose favourite toy was a piece of string.

Typeset by Avonset, Midsomer Norton, Avon
Printed in Great Britain by Redwood Press Ltd, Melksham, Wilts

# CONTENTS

# ACKNOWLEDGEMENTS

I am grateful to XM Yachting for supplying me with samples of Liros Yacht Ropes, and particularly to Ian McCormack for his enthusiastic assistance and splicing tips. Also to Peter Plumb of Roblon (UK) for the personal visit and the subsequent samples. Marlow Ropes provided many of the ropes used in the photographs, and Marilyn Kitcher furnished the latest available information on the new fibres.

Thank you to Mike Roff of Bridon Ropes Ltd, Des Pawson of Footrope Knots, David Warren of Marine Instruments, and Reg Langdon Marine of Truro.

The ropes in the coiling sequences all belong to Phil Samuel's Trapper 300.

Finally, I must thank Gordon T, my first and only helmsman. Tyrant, husband, yacht designer extraordinaire, he tolerated the reduced culinary and domestic state whilst I was writing this book, without a murmur.

# INTRODUCTION

My initiation into the rudiments of knot tying proper (as opposed to a jumble of granny knots imparting a somewhat spurious sense of security) came about during my schooldays when I took up dinghy sailing.

My helmsman was a tyrant, and I soon learned that there is the right knot for the job, particularly when it comes to *untying* it, and there is a preferred method of tying for speed and accuracy. There's nothing like watching your jib sheet disappear through the block whilst hurtling along on a Tornado to make you wish you had brushed up on your stopper knots the night before!

It became apparent that if I wanted to carry on crewing, I would have to learn quickly or risk being jettisoned overboard, so I went in search of some sort of instruction manual. I found *Reed's Nautical Almanac* and began to practise.

When I had perfected the dozen or so knots, bends and hitches in Reed's, I carried on through splices, whipping and the rest of the Almanac.

I was still hungry for knots, and started looking around for something a little more taxing. It was at about this time that I began working in the photographic field. My colleague was a modern-day ex-merchant seaman with a nautical turn of phrase (we didn't have floors, just decks!) and a wide repertoire of knots. And so began my apprenticeship in square knotting.

This was something to really get my teeth into (literally) and I graduated to what is now known as macramé, the practice of which can reward you with items of exquisite beauty, and the hands of an old sea dog.

When you have mastered all the utility knots, and can whip and splice with the best of them, you may like to try some of the decorative items with which to adorn your craft, your home, or even your loyal friends, who will wonder how they ever got along without a knotted winch-handle pocket.

I have tried to illustrate as clearly as possible, with photographs and diagrams, the stages of each knot in order that you can form any one without having to wade through acres of text, deciphering instructions with one eye and watching your hands with the other. This is very bad for the eyes – and the patience.

The written instructions are there mainly as a back-up to explain any difficult points, and you may also find it useful to rope in a friend to read them out while you grapple with the action.

Inevitably, there are a few terms to remember, and I cover these before the real knot tying begins in earnest.

The approach to some of the methods may be somewhat unorthodox (what do you do with eight cans of beans and 20 metres of rope?) but the objective is to make it easy . . . and fun!

# A Note on Knots

Knots, as a method of fastening strands of stuff together, are not necessarily of purely nautical beginnings. They originate from all parts of the world, and from many vocations – weavers, truck drivers, surgeons, climbers, to name a few.

The sailor has been known to take any method of forming a knot which is easier to remember or easier to tie, and adopt it as a preferred method. It has to be said though, that the merchant sailors of old were the most prolific of rope workers, and it is they who must be credited with the more complex decorative knotting, buttons and sinnet work.

A knot is generally classified according to its use, hence a *bend* is used to join or bend two ropes together, a *hitch* secures a rope to a post, eye or hook, and a *knot* is usually used to make a *loop* or a *stopper*, but the nomenclature of knots is inconsistent, to say the least, so I have tended to avoid ambiguous grouping.

Instead, I have tried to include all the knots which would be most useful, in order of prominence, aboard a small sailing cruiser, keel boat or sailing dinghy, since this is where you are likely to find the need for a selection of knots to cope with different situations.

This of course is open to argument as there are those who favour one or two knots above all others and use them exclusively, no matter what the task. This can be somewhat risky, as some knots are completely unsuitable in certain situations and can be dangerous to life and craft.

I urge you to practise all the knots in this book – or at least the utility knots – and become proficient in putting them to their correct use. Apart from the safety aspect, it is very satisfying to come alongside at the marina, smiling at your next-berth neighbour whilst nonchalantly forming a double Matthew Walker with one hand, and twirling a Crown Sinnet-covered fender in the other. This is boat credibility with a capital 'C'!

Though knots are quick and easy to make, they do weaken the rope in which they are tied. Where the rope is bent around in a tight turn it has to distort considerably, which puts the fibres around the outside of the turn under considerable tension, and those on the inside under compression. The rope flattens out to adapt to the changes, which deforms the fibres even more.

When a knot fails under load, the reaction is tremendous. Whilst pulling up a tree stump, using a hollow braided polyester rope of about 18mm diameter tied to a car, the rope failed just outside the bowline tied around the stump. The recoiling rope removed a 200mm (8in) line of paintwork from a second car standing close by. It is important that there are no more people than absolutely necessary in the vicinity of any rope under heavy load, and for those present to keep well clear. They would not want their paintwork removed!

Knot strength cannot easily be calculated – there are many variables, particularly with the modern polymer-based ropes, but it is prudent to be aware of the inherent weakness in knots, and replace them with splices wherever possible.

**SUMMARY**

- Knots weaken the rope in which they are tied; the failure point on a rope is always at the knot.

- Use splices in preference to knots wherever possible.

- Observe the safety rules: keep well clear of ropes under heavy loads.

# 1

# ROPE MATERIALS AND CONSTRUCTION

I don't intend to regale you with the history of ropemaking, nor dazzle you with the molecular science of modern synthetics – there are numerous books which can do that quite admirably.

What I will do is run through the most commonly available ropes, and some not so common ones, and tell you a little about their construction, enough to enable you to understand their strengths and weaknesses, and how they differ when it comes to knotting, splicing and general usage.

I make no apology for using brand names where appropriate, but it is unlikely that you will find all of them in one chandlery store.

The first point to grasp is that the material from which a rope is made is the primary determining factor in the use to which it is put. For example, you do not use nylon for halyards if you do not favour baggy luffs; nor do you use Kevlar to attach your fenders unless you have more money than sense.

Here is a rundown of man made fibres used in ropemaking today, but with the perpetual advance in materials technology, it is possible that by the time you read this there will be other permutations on the market as the manufacturers compete in their quest to produce stronger, lighter, higher performance rope.

## Materials

### Polyester

You may be familiar with some of the trade names – Terylene, Dacron, Tergal, Fortrel. Polyester is the one from which the majority of sheets and halyards are made. It has a lower stretch factor than nylon, and is also available in pre-stretched and super pre-stretched. It comes in lots of jolly colours, including neons.

All the manufacturers supply a similar range of polyester ropes – braid on braid, three-strand, 8-plait, 16-plait with a matt finish, pre-stretched. In addition Liros have an amazing range of neons and rainbow checks which would look wicked on a sailboard, and Marlow make a three-strand super pre-stretched suitable for halyards, instead of wire. If you are not into rainbow hues, Roblon make an absolutely plain white halyard – not a fleck to be seen.

### Nylon

The trade names: Polyamide, Bri-nylon, Enkalon. It is cheaper than polyester and extremely strong. The fact that it is very stretchy makes it good for mooring and anchor warps, though useless for sheets and halyards. Any colour you like as long as it's white. Tends to come as plaited rope – 'Octoplait' from Liros, 'Multiplait' from Marlow, and 'Squareline' from Bridon Ropes.

## Polypropylene

Polypropylene is relatively cheap but has about half the breaking strength of nylon. It is very susceptible to abrasion and if not protected from chafe, it will wear itself out fairly quickly. The better quality polypropylenes are stabilized against the sun's ultraviolet rays which lead to degradation, but cheap imitations not meant for marine use will deteriorate in sunlight; so buy from a reputable source.

There are two advantages to this fibre – it is lightweight and it floats. At one time it was available only in garish orange, shades of blue and a translucent white, like Marlow Nelson, but there are now braided polypropylenes like Marlow's Marstron in five colours, which are suitable for dinghy sheets, and Roblon manufacture a black braided polypropylene called Multiflex, and a lightweight spinnaker sheet in double braided polypropylene available in red and blue.

Due to a demand for traditional hemp lookalikes, it is also being manufactured in shades of brown, some smooth, some with a soft hairy finish. This makes it more aesthetically suitable for use on classic boats and square riggers, provided the strength characteristics are allowed for. Liros 'Synthemp' and Marlow 'Hardyhemp' are both pale and hairy. Roblon 'Spunflex', a darker brown, is slightly shiny to begin with but dulls to an interesting 'old rope' finish.

## Aramid Fibres

Universally referred to as Kevlar, though strictly this is a trade name. It is not, as is often thought, a carbon fibre. It was developed by Du Pont in America some years ago and is an organic polymer, immune to moisture and rot, with a very high strength to weight ratio. Its stretch characteristics are close to those of $1 \times 19$ stainless steel wire, and it is often used to replace wire halyards to effect a weight advantage. It certainly lightens your bank account! The disadvantages are not inconsiderable – it has a marked inability to stand flexing; the fibres are brittle and tend to destroy each other. Care must be taken with sheave diameters and cleating. The fibres will not stand abrasion and are sensitive to ultraviolet light. For these reasons they are always contained within an outer sheath of polyester.

Liros make a Kevlar-cored rope, as do Marlow (KT3) and Roblon produce a halyard with an inner braid of part Kevlar, part polyester. 'Marina Hystrain' Kevlar is offered by Bridon Ropes.

## The New Breed

A greater flex fatigue life than aramids; high strength to weight ratio; extremely low stretch: these are the manufacturers' claims for their new progeny. There are two names to be considered so far: 'Dyneema' from the Far East, and its American counterpart from Allied called 'Spectra' or HMPE which stands for High Modulus Polyethylene.

This new generation would seem to offer more than the Kevlar brood, but at a higher price. It can be knotted without crippling the fibres, and it can be cut and heat sealed. On larger diameters, the inner

9

core is enclosed in a soft gauze-like sheath, which can cause a few headaches when splicing (not recommended for the amateur). Liros call theirs 'Dyneema', Marlow stick with 'Spectra', and Roblon have named theirs 'Admiral 2000', which is based on Spectra.

## Construction

There are three basic types of construc-
tion: three-strand, braided and multiplait (*see* Fig 1).

## *Three-strand*

This is self-explanatory. Fibre bundles are spun into strands and three strands are twisted together to make three-strand, usually with a right-handed lay, that is, with the strands spiralling clockwise away from you.

It is very easy to splice.

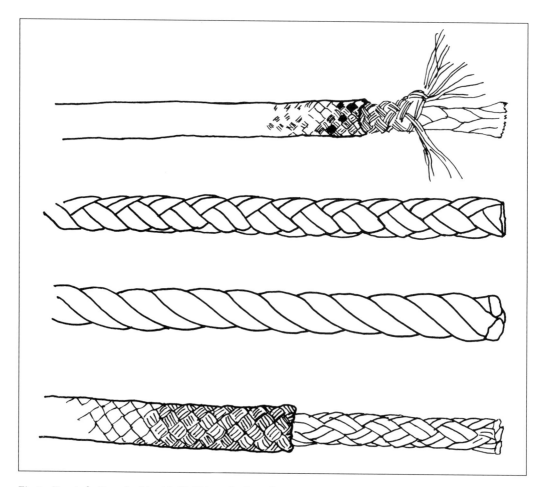

Fig 1    Top to bottom: braid with HMPE; multiplait; three-strand; braid on braid.

## Braided

The term *braided rope* covers several different constructions. The most common is a braided outer sheathing over a braided inner core. Another has a braided outer sheathing over a parallel multifilament core, or a three-strand core. Also available are braided ropes with a Kevlar core, and lastly, to date, are the new breed of braided ropes which have their shiny core fibres, also braided, encased in a thin matt sheathing, all encased in an outer sheathing. The outers are usually made from sixteen or eight strands plaited together. This makes for soft and comfortable handling characteristics. Braided polypropylenes are also becoming more common, and these are of hollow construction.

## Multiplait

This is constructed with eight fat strands woven in pairs, like a solid sinnet. It is mostly of nylon, very soft and stretchy. Because of its construction it does not form kinks, making it suitable for anchor warps.

You will find more information on construction in the splicing section under the pertinent headings.

---

**SUMMARY**

Choose materials to suit the job in hand:

- Polyester is a low-stretch fibre.

- Nylon is strong and stretchy.

- Polypropylene is cheap, light and buoyant.

- Aramids are high strength and high price.

---

# 2
# WHAT TO USE WHERE

Choosing suitable rope for the various tasks on a boat is a daunting prospect, especially when confronted with the huge range of fibres and finishes now available.

This is an attempt at simplifying the choice by giving some guidelines for use when you venture into the chandlers.

There are basically three different functions for rope to fulfil on board, be it sailing dinghy, keel boat, narrowboat or cruiser. These are sheets, halyards and mooring ropes. Let's take them one at a time.

## Sheets

The primary criterion for a sheet is handling comfort. A sheet has to be user friendly, which is why dinghy sailors do not have to worry about breaking strengths – with modern ropes, an adequate size to satisfy the strength criterion would be too thin for comfortable handling. The usual size is 8–10mm, with about 6mm for spinnaker sheets.

Keel boats have to think a little more carefully about breaking strengths and all reputable rope manufacturers and importers supply useful literature with information on sizes and strengths. As a rough guide, a 12–14m (40–45ft) sailing boat would use a mainsheet size of 12mm, genoa probably 14mm and spinnaker 12mm, though a serious racer would probably go for a high-strength rope with a smaller diameter to save weight.

The preferred fibre would be polyester, but the choice does not stop there. Polyester ropes are available in a variety of forms and finishes. Three-strand is shiny and hard on the hands, so is not normally used for sheets. It also tends to kink which can be a problem where blocks and fairleads are concerned.

A braided rope is the usual choice, and the finish depends on personal preference. Of the matt finishes, Marlow 16-plait is marginally softer than Liros 16-plait. The Roblon Mastersheet is harder, so may distort less under pressure from cleats and stoppers.

There is a vast selection of shiny braided rope, the most exciting of which come from Liros and would be particularly attractive to board sailors. These include the vivid rainbow checks and neons – all very high profile. There are more refined patterns available from the same stable, as well as from other manufacturers. All are soft to handle and not too difficult to splice.

Of course there is also Kevlar, and an interesting one here is the Marlow matt

Kevlar, KT3 core with a matt polyester braided cover. The outer braid can be pushed back and cut off, leaving a thinner polyester braid covering a Kevlar core. Whip the taper point and you have a lightweight spinnaker sheet with a soft handle tail on it for cockpit handling.

Both Roblon and Liros have a matt Kevlar, and Liros also has a shiny one. All offer extremely low stretch.

Just to add further to the choice, there is a new fibre on the market (*see* Chapter 1, page 8). Available as 'Admiral 2000' from Roblon, 'Spectra' from Marlow and 'Dyneema' from Liros, it is suitable as sheets if you can afford it.

## Halyards

As you can see from the foregoing, there is a wide range from which to choose your sheets, but with halyards there is the added complication of braided versus three strand.

Both have their advantages. Three strand is resistant to abrasion and it holds its cross-sectional shape well. It is also cheaper than braided rope. It is available in a limited range of whites, and the pre-stretched is suitable for halyards. Marlow's super pre-stretched is marketed as a replacement for wire halyards.

Braided rope is possibly the more popular choice, especially on racing yachts. There are Roblon's 'Standard' and 'Master Halyard', Liros 'Braid on Braid' and Marlow's 'Marlowbraid', plus their 8-plait pre-stretched for dinghy halyards. 'Super Braidline' comes from Bridon Ropes.

Then there are the Kevlars and the HMPEs which come into their own in the wire replacement field.

Again, for a 12–14m (40–45ft) yacht, a diameter of 12mm would be suitable all round, and one size down for the mighty fibres.

Given the range of colours and designs on the market, colour coding is simplicity itself.

## Mooring

Every boat has to be moored up or anchored at some time, and it is prudent to carry the right types of rope to make a proper job of it. You may not foresee every problem you are likely to encounter during mooring, but of one thing you can be sure – the eyes and bollards in your chosen port will be in positions and at spacings which bear no relation to your lines whatsoever.

The primary objective whilst alongside is to keep your boat from being damaged. That means preventing drift fore and aft, and avoiding repeated contact with the dockside. The most useful lines are probably those which run respectively from the bow to a mooring point aft, and from the quarter to a point forward. These are called *springs* and they prevent the boat from surging fore and aft and help to keep it parallel to the quay. *Bow lines* and *stern lines* can be added if you are staying alongside for any length of time. They are also referred to as 'head and stern lines' or 'bow and stern ropes', and are led from the bow forward and from the stern aft. They assist in checking fore and aft movement and keep the ends in position (*see* Fig 2).

Length calculations for mooring ropes have to take into account the vagaries of dockside bollard positions and tidal ranges, as well as the possibilities of

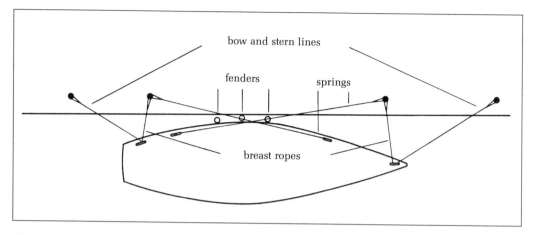

Fig 2   Mooring ropes.

rafting in crowded ports (lying alongside other boats possibly three and four deep) so it is preferable to err on the long side.

A rough estimate would be one-and-a-half boat lengths per spring and twice the boat length for bow and stern lines. Obviously you will have other lines on board which can be utilized if extra length is required.

In a marina situation, where the pontoons rise and fall with the boats, you are unlikely to need bow and stern lines, but you can substitute *breast ropes* to assist the springs. These are shorter lines laid approximately at right angles to the boat to stop the ends drifting outwards. You could use your bow and stern lines, but there will be an awfully large pile of loose rope lying around.

The obvious choice for dock lines is nylon. Because of its elasticity, it will absorb the loads applied by wind and water, not to mention Bacchanalian revellers clambering across your foredeck at three o' clock in the morning on their way to the last boat on the raft.

There is an optimum size for dock lines

– too small and . . . 'ping' . . . the obvious will happen, too large and you will lose the stretch advantage. (A light boat on a heavy line does not exert enough force to bring the elasticity into play.) Our hypothetical 12–14m yacht, given a displacement of about 10 tonnes, would be happy on 16mm dock lines of nylon.

Put Eye Splices in one end of all your dock lines. This is the end which you heave at all and sundry on the dock, and the fact that a lot of them won't know a bowline from a banana doesn't matter because anyone can put an eye over a bollard.

You must be vigilant about chafe on mooring lines, particularly if you have two lines through one cleat where they will try to wear each other out. Plastic hose is a must here.

There is an interesting ready-made mooring line available from Roblon which is of black braided nylon with a built-in 40cm (16in) rubber sausage which acts as a shock absorber. The line comes in three diameters and two lengths. It is equipped with a plastic sleeve, a wire splicing tool

Fig 3   Roblon readymade mooring line with built-in spring.

Fig 4   It's the lead that makes the difference – 48lb on the scales.

and a set of instructions in Danish, but the pictures are very easy to follow (*see* Fig 3).

The last thing you need to know about mooring alongside is that you will always need one more fender than you have on board. That is one of the laws of the sea.

# Anchor Warps

High strength, elasticity and no-kink tendencies are all called for in an anchor warp, and that rather points to a nylon multiplait. It can be spliced directly to chain and is soft to handle even when wet.

A three-strand polyester would fulfil the strength criterion, and would stand up better to chafe and abrasion, but it can kink and it needs to be spliced into an eye and shackled onto the chain.

There is a product on the market which claims to eliminate the need for chain, and would perhaps be suitable for the smaller keel boats. It is a polyester line with lead built in to the first 12m (40ft). It comes in a plastic bucket, in several sizes, from Roblon. It is also available in a less expensive polypropylene version. As an example, the 50m-length (160ft) braided line weighs 21.5kg (47lb) with 15kg (33lb) of lead inserted (*see* Fig 4).

---

**SUMMARY**

- Sheets: Choose braided polyester for handling comfort and strength.

- Halyards: Polyester again, for its low-stretch properties, or Kevlar and HMPE if the budget allows.

- Mooring: Nylon, strong and stretchy.

---

# 3
# TOOLS

To tie knots you need only one tool, and that is a pair of hands. In some cases, even this can be reduced to one hand, in which case teeth often come into play.

But there are a few extra tools you will find useful when splicing, whipping and seizing. Some are specialized and will have to be begged, borrowed or bought, but some you may have already in your tool box.

1   *A good sharp knife.* This can be a pukka 'yachtsman's knife' which folds up when not in use, or a broad-bladed straight knife in a sheath, often available with other tools in a set which attaches to your belt. Whichever you choose, keep it sharp with a small carborundum stone, also kept in your kit (*see* Fig 5).

2   *A marline spike*, often attached to said 'yachtsman's knife' but preferably not, as it is likely you will need to use both ends at the same time, and this can be detrimental to the welfare of the fingers. A spike attached to a shackle key is quite comfortable to use, or one of traditional pattern with a wooden handle. The spike is used to part the strands of wire or rope when splicing, to tighten up turns when seizing and to open up knots which are jammed.

3   *Fids* are used in the same way as a marline spike when splicing rope. Traditional fids are made from hard woods such as lignum vitae, ash and rosewood. These are useful on larger-diameter ropes, and are very pleasant to handle. Modern versions in synthetic materials are equally effective and they are cheap, but they don't have that 'old salt' feel. At the other extreme, I have a set of quite beautiful stainless-steel hollow tube fids from Norway which are extremely neat, easy to use, and undoubtedly destined for many a yachtsman's toolkit. If you just want something cheap and cheerful to do the odd braid splice, then Roblon sell a set of blue plastic hollow knitting needles, perfectly adequate for the job (*see* Fig 6).

4   *A hollow spike*, also called a Swedish pattern fid, is useful when splicing anything fiddly, as the strands can be tucked through with the spike in place.

5   *Small pliers* come in handy to pull through strands, also to grasp a needle when fingers can't get a grip. Stainless steel is the obvious choice of material, but

Fig 5   A popular tool set for yachtsmen.

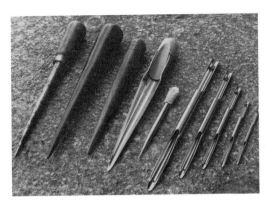

Fig 6   Spikes and fids.

Fig 7   Sewing requisites.

in my experience they are usually steel, in shades of oil and rust.

6 *Sailmaker's palm.* This is an interesting piece of essential equipment for use when whipping, worn like a glove without fingers, back or cuff. Made of hide, it has a dimpled metal insert which lies over the heel of the thumb, by which the needle is pushed through the work, always away from the body, in a kind of 'gripping' action. Some palms are of a broader pattern to protect the edge of the hand when pulling taut the thread. Available left- or right-handed (*see* Fig 7).

7 *Needles* for whipping and sewing should be of the sailmaker's pattern, which differs from common sewing needles in that the section is triangular for part of the length. You will need various sizes depending on size of thread used, which should go through the eye comfortably. Keep your needles stuck in a cork and carried in a tin, or use a short stainless-steel tube with a rubber bung in each end.

8 *Whipping twine* is used for a multitude of purposes, apart from whipping and seizing. It is available in different sizes and colours. You will find the waxed type

easier to use, but you can also wax your own if you keep a block of beeswax in your kit.

9 *Tape* of various descriptions is really useful to have around when working with rope. Masking tape, plastic electrical tape, fabric tape, Sellotape – any or all of these are worth using to bind the strands of rope when splicing, if you don't have the time or the inclination to whip them. Tape can also be used as a temporary measure to wrap the end of a rope, pending a back-splice or a proper whipping. Anything which prevents your ends unlaying is good news.

10 *A butane lighter*, whether you smoke or not, could be considered an essential piece of equipment. It melts the fibres of synthetic ropes without leaving a black deposit, unlike ordinary matches. The melted fibres tend to make a blob on the end of the rope, but if you roll it between two pieces of wood while it is still hot, it will become the same diameter as the rope. You may see people licking their fingers and using them to shape the hot blob – this is not recommended on anything but small stuff, unless you have ceramic fingertips.

It is not necessary to spend vast sums of money on specialist tools when a perfectly good substitute can be made in the workshop, or discovered in markets and junk shops.

It is possible to utilize all manner of common items when knotting and splicing. Double-ended knitting needles come in handy when braid splicing, as do pieces of copper or aluminium tube, angled and smoothed at one end.

A tip from Ian McCormack is to use the outer casings of ball point pens as hollow fids. They are especially useful when threading wire through braided cores. You could also use them when splicing with heat-sealed ends, which tend to catch in the fibres as you tuck them.

Crochet hooks and rug-making latchet hooks are effective when working decorative knots in small stuff.

---

**SUMMARY**

- Aim for a set of high-quality tools, but in the beginning you can improvize.

- The absolute minimum requirement on board would be a good knife, a spike and a pair of pliers, plus needles and twine for repairs.

# 4
# TERMINOLOGY

So, you are standing on a pontoon in the marina at St Moritz tanned, sophisticated and minding your own business, when a smart 12-metre (40ft) yacht heads in to berth at that very pontoon. The suave helmsman throws you a line and calls, 'Take a turn around that cleat could you?' Well, that seems easy enough, and you loop the line around the cleat and stand there with the end of the rope dangling from your fingers as the yacht comes to a gentle halt. Mr Smoothy, recognizing your prowess with a rope, requests, 'Perhaps you could just put in a bowline and hitch it onto the cleat so I can take up the slack.' OK. Do you run? Do you stand there gaping? Do you panic? Of course you don't, because you have spent the winter avidly reading this book and a bowline is second nature to you. You even tie them in the dark!

You take the *standing part*, form a *bight* in the *working part* and do a few clever things with the *bitter end* and miraculously, a bowline appears. You put the eye through the cleat and over the horns, and signal the skipper to take in the line. You are confident and secure in the knowledge that your performance was impeccable, and the yacht is not about to come adrift due to any ineptitude on your part.

These age old terms to describe the different parts of a rope are illustrated in Fig 8, but you will find I have used slight variations throughout the book. The term

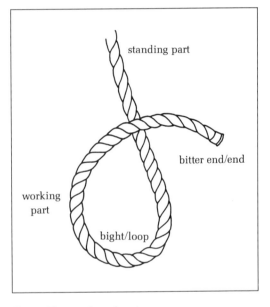

Fig 8   The naming of parts.

*bight* can be used to mean either the slack part of the rope between the standing part and the end when it forms a curve, or it can mean the space or loop which is formed. To avoid confusion, I have tended to use the word *loop* when you are about to feed the end through.

The *standing part* is the (usually longer) part coming from a fixed point.

The *bitter end* is self-explanatory and traditionally correct, but is referred to throughout as the *end* for brevity.

The *working part* is the part you are handling during the knot-forming exercises.

# TERMINOLOGY

The *lay* of the rope refers to the direction of the twist in a three-strand rope. Those you will find in the chandler's are likely to be of right-hand lay, that is, the three strands spiral away from you in a clockwise direction. 'Opening the lay' means parting the strands, as when splicing.

This is really all you need to remember, and you will find it easy to pick up as you go along. You can also refer to the Glossary (page 126) when necessary.

**SUMMARY**

*Bight* – loop.

*Working part* – the bit you are knotting.

*Standing part* – the bit that isn't doing anything.

*End* – the end you are playing with.

# 5
# THE KNOTS

One of the first things to know about a knot is the way it looks. The act of tying a knot is secondary to the ability to see the finished article *in your head*.

It is worth studying the photographs and diagrams to impinge the image on to your brain. If you can visualize the completed knot before you begin to tie it, you are half way to tying it correctly.

Follow the instructions by all means, but don't get bogged down by detail – don't lose that image.

If your visual perception is on the weak side, then you may have to apply more concentration to the knot, but eventually it will come. You will tie that knot because you *know* that knot.

I suggest you begin by acquiring a length of good-quality rope, say 9–10mm diameter. The length is not important, but you need to fix one end to a solid object, like a desk leg, radiator or door handle, and sit comfortably about two metres away from the fixing point, with about a metre of rope to play with. You can attach the rope with a couple of granny knots. If you can't find a solid object take your trusty length of rope and tie it around your foot.

And now we can begin.

## The Bowline

There are umpteen ways to tie a Bowline, depending on the purpose and situation, and it is not necessary to illustrate all of them. (You may not mind being hauled up the mast by your armpits, but I prefer the bosun's chair, or even better a dry dock with monster crane, so you won't find a Spanish Bowline here.)

The Bowline is first because it is just about the most useful knot on board. If properly formed it will not slip, jam or capsize, and yet it is easy to untie. It is used for forming a loop in the end of a rope; as a hitch when attaching a painter to a ring; for attaching jib sheets to the clew of the foresail; for attaching lanyards to anything; as a bend when joining two ropes. It can also be seized for extra security, which will be explained later in the book.

### Method

To enable the procedure to be more easily remembered, I present The Bunny Rabbit Method. (Of course, you still have to remember that the end of the rope is the rabbit and the standing part is the tree!)

So, decide how large a loop you need. Allow about three times the length of the finished loop and begin the knot there (i.e. if you want a loop of 30cm (12in), begin the knot approximately 90cm (36in) from the end).

Make a loop – or a rabbit hole – with the standing part underneath.

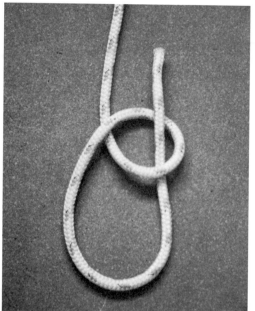

Fig 9   Bunny up through hole.

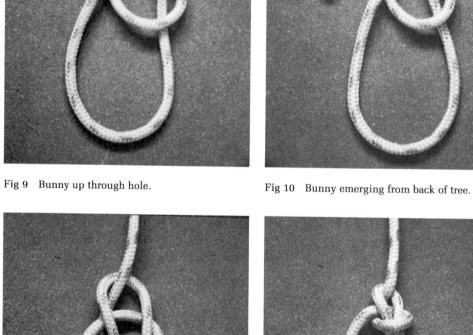

Fig 10   Bunny emerging from back of tree.

Fig 11   Bunny bolting down hole.

Fig 12   Bunny snug in burrow.

Lead the rabbit up through the hole (*see* Fig 9) around the back of the tree (*see* Fig 10) and back down the hole (*see* Fig 11).

Draw the end up carefully to make a close knot.

You have now made a Bowline (*see* Fig 12). If you haven't, take another look at the diagrams, in case your bunny went the wrong way.

The *second option* is more difficult to describe, and involves forming the hole around the rabbit. Hold the standing part in the left hand and the end in the right, making a 'U' shape, palms towards you (*see* Fig 13).

Hold the end up and wind the standing part around it in an anticlockwise direction (*see* Fig 14). You now have a bunny coming up through the hole, just as in the first mode. Send him around the tree and down the hole – *voilà*, another perfect bowline, and slightly quicker.

There is a *third option* which is of use when the Bowline is to be tied around a fixed object, like a ring or a mooring eye. This is easier with soft rope but you won't necessarily have a choice in the matter, so just persevere. You will have to change position for this, or use another piece of rope and put it through something so that *both* ends are coming towards you.

It will be described with the standing part on the left, the short working end on the right, but you will have to *cross your hands left over right* before grasping the rope parts (*see* Fig 15).

Take the end in your left hand, bring it back over, round and through the standing part (which you are holding in your right hand). This makes a Half Hitch (*see* Fig 16).

Now here's the tricky bit – push *away* and slightly to the left with your right hand, and *pull towards you* with your left (*see* Fig 17). This changes the form of the

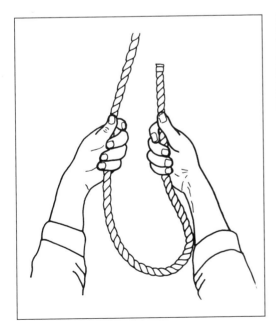

Fig 13   Make a 'U' shape.

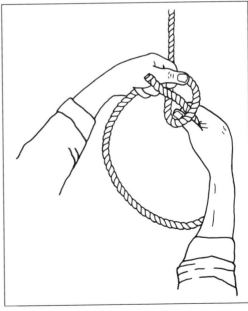

Fig 14   Wind anticlockwise.

23

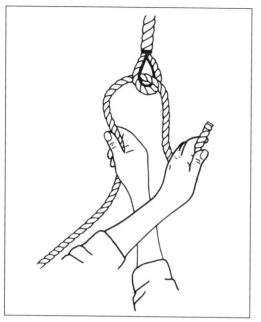

Fig 15   Cross your hands first.

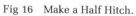

Fig 16   Make a Half Hitch.

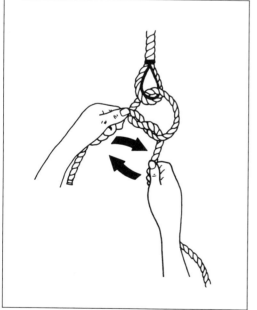

Fig 17   Push with right and pull with left.

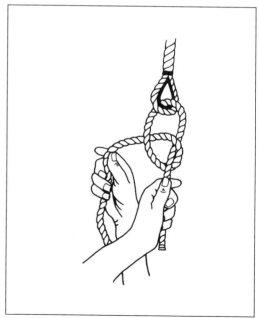

Fig 18   Here comes bunny.

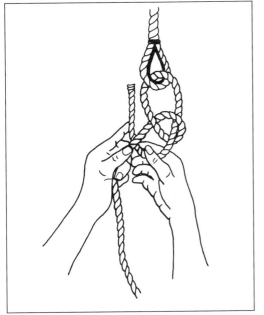

Fig 19   Around the tree . . .

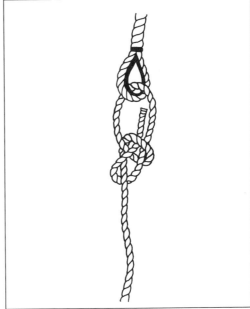

Fig 20   . . . and through the hole.

knot, and with a bit of luck you have just made yet another rabbit hole, complete with resident bunny already emerging (*see* Fig 18). But remember, the tree is upside down, with the top towards you, so send him around the back from right to left (*see* Fig 19) and down the hole again (*see* Fig 20).

That makes *three* different ways you now know of tying a Bowline. The only other thing you need to know is how to untie it. Basically, you turn the knot over and push the rabbit's behind up the tree, which loosens the whole warren, enabling you to dismantle it (*see* Fig 21).

When using a Bowline to attach the sheets to the genoa, make the loop fairly short, or you may find that the knot will foul the block, preventing the genoa from being fully sheeted.

Fig 21   Rear view – push upwards to loosen.

# Half Hitch

Let's go back to that Half Hitch which you unwittingly but so deftly made during your foray into Bowlines. The Half Hitch offers no security whatsoever when used on its own. It is usually one of the steps in making other knots, and it is very, very easy.

## *Method*

Starting with the rope as you left it, around an object such as a spar or a ring (or in your case, a table leg) with both ends coming towards you, take the short end across and around the standing part and up through the space or hole you have just formed (*see* Fig 22).

Keep the standing part taut while you execute the hitch. If the action is repeated, you will have two Half Hitches (*see* Fig 23) or even more if you get carried away.

You will come across it again in the decorative knotting section (*see* Chapter 12, page 89).

Fig 22   First Half Hitch.

Fig 23   Two Half Hitches.

## Round Turn and Two Half Hitches

While we are on the subject of hitches, let us cover the Turn, the Round Turn, and the ubiquitous Round Turn and two Half Hitches.

A Turn is executed by wrapping the rope 360 degrees around an object, so that the end still points in the direction it held before the turn (see Fig 24). This is of use if you are on the pontoon/quay having been thrown a line from a slow-moving craft with the request to 'take a turn' around a cleat/bollard. The friction in the turn makes it very easy to take the strain. By utilizing this friction, the line can be 'paid out' gradually, as in bow and stern lines when mooring, or it can be unwound and let go immediately, as when leaving a berth.

A Round Turn is, in effect, a turn and a half, but we won't quibble about the extra 180 degrees. It results in both ends pointing in the same direction (see Fig 24). This gives even more friction, as you will know if you have any experience with winches – two or three turns of a sheet on a winch give more control than just one.

The Round Turn is also the first step in making several other knots, including the Round Turn and Two Half Hitches (see Fig 25). You already know how to do the latter part so it should take you a few seconds to put the two parts together. You can use it to secure the dinghy painter to a mooring eye, or to tie up alongside on a post or bollard.

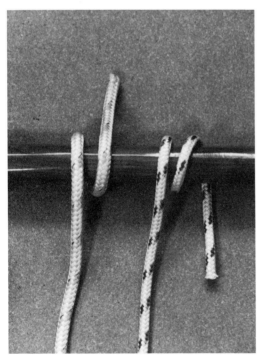

Fig 24   A Turn and a Round Turn.

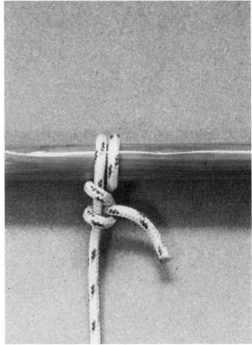

Fig 25   Round Turn and two Half Hitches.

# Fisherman's Bend/Anchor Bend

A variation on the Round Turn and two Half Hitches is the Fisherman's Bend, also known as the Anchor Bend, for the simple reason that it is a very secure way of attaching a warp to an anchor (or, presumably, to a fisherman).

The first stage is a Round Turn on the anchor shackle or ring, as in Fig 26 (this is when you have progressed from the table leg); then form the first Half Hitch around the standing part but *tuck the end through the round turn* as well (*see* Fig 27). Work it tight, then put on the second Half Hitch, as per normal, in the same direction.

For more assured security in use, the end should be seized to the standing part (*see* Fig 28).

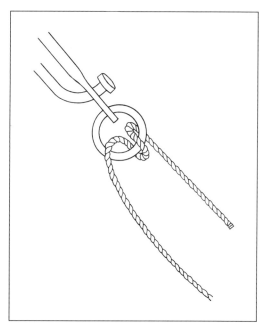

Fig 26   Make a Round Turn.

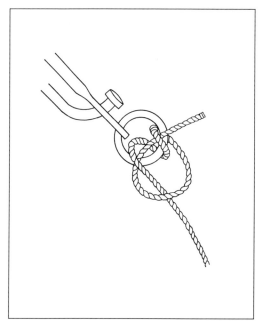

Fig 27   Tuck through Round Turn as well.

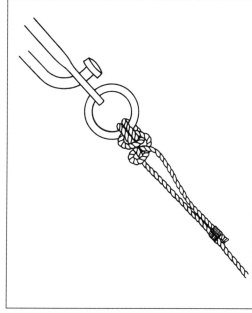

Fig 28   Seize for security.

# Clove Hitch

In the days when life jackets resembled inflatable oranges, and buoyancy came in bags, no self respecting dinghy sailor ventured forth without a burgee (rectangular for racing, triangular for cruising) complete with its own burgee halyard, often made from whipping twine spliced into a continuous loop, and with its own miniature cleat on the mast. The way of attaching the burgee prior to hoisting was with two Clove Hitches, about 15cm (6in) apart on the burgee stick, which ensured it stayed upright and raised above the top of the mast. The same arrangement applied to bigger boats, the halyard usually being of codline (pronounced cod-lin), a three-stranded cord made of hemp. Since the advent of wind vanes in assorted sizes for small and large boats, plus the mind boggling array of electronic wind speed and direction indicators now available, the burgee halyard has all but disappeared from modern craft.

However, the Clove Hitch is still extremely useful, not least for attaching your fenders to the guard rails (*see* Fig 29).

## Method

You will need a horizontal pole or rope stretched between two points. With your piece of practice rope in a vertical position, take a turn around the stand-in guard rail, with the end on the right (i.e. a clockwise turn coming towards you if viewed from the right (*see* Fig 30)). Form a Half Hitch, in the same direction, to the *left* of the turn (*see* Figs 31, 32).

You should now have a Clove Hitch. It is worth practising this over and over until you can do it without thinking. It is very

Fig 29   Fender attached with slipped Clove Hitch.

easy to make the second hitch the wrong way.

To make the slipped Clove Hitch, do not put the end through when making the second Half Hitch, but tuck through a loop and pull tight.

Fig 30　Take a turn.

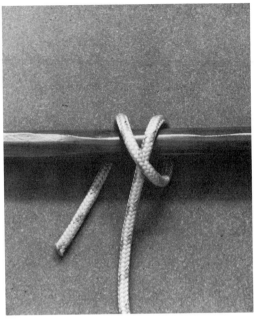

Fig 31　Over and round.

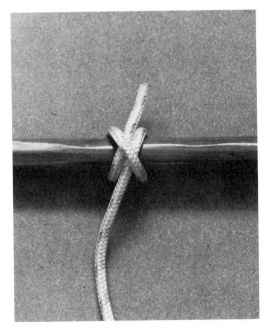

Fig 32　Clove Hitch completed.

A variation is to form the complete Hitch in your hands first. This is useful on board for slipping over the tiller; then the ends are cleated off at the quarters, keeping the rudder central, or at the required angle whilst on the mooring.

The method is quick and requires no 'threading through' of ends. Make a clockwise loop in the rope, as if you were starting to coil it (*see* Fig 33). Hold this in your left hand, then make another loop and hold it in your right hand (*see* Fig 34). This gives you two identical 'coil loops', one in your left hand, one in your right. Now, here's the magic bit – slip the right hand coil behind the left until the coils lie together, one in front of the other (*see* Fig 35). The whole Hitch is then slipped over the end of the tiller and tightened, cleating the ends as described (*see* Fig 36).

DILLONS THE BOOKSTORE
82 GOWER STREET
LONDON
WC1E 6EQQ

D064
NATURAL HISTORY AND P    £25.00
1852237058
KNOTS AND ROPE WORK       £8.99
                 TOT:    £33.99

F2    CHEQUE AMT:          £33.99
Card No:9198936M5
REC:   7929:240793:1708:18ACHA
    PLEASE RETAIN FOR REFERENCE
    VAT No. 486 922 011

# d

**Dillons The Bookstore**
82 Gower Street
London WCI 6EQ
Telephone: 071 636 1577

Registered office:
Pentos Retailing Group Limited
35 Livery Street Birmingham B3 2PB
VAT Reg. No. 486 9220 11

# dˢ

**Dillons The Bookstore**
82 Gower Street
London WCI 6EQ
Telephone: 071 636 1577

Registered office:
Pentos Retailing Group Limited
35 Livery Street Birmingham B3 2PB

Fig 33   Make a clockwise loop in left hand.

Fig 34   Another clockwise loop in right hand.

Fig 35   Slip right coil behind left coil.

Fig 36   Slip Clove Hitch over the end.

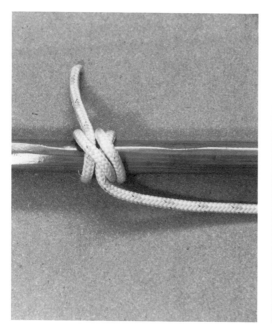

Fig 37   Rolling Hitch.

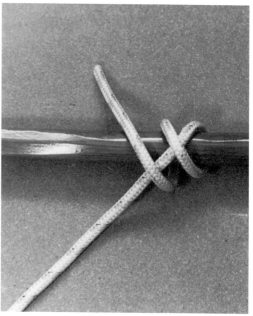

Fig 38   Include the standing part.

Fig 39   Turn and tuck.

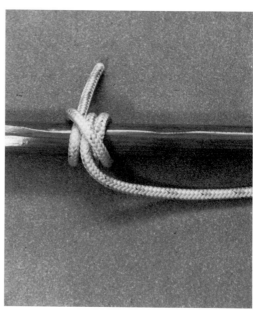

Fig 40   Alternative Rolling Hitch for smooth surface.

# Rolling Hitch

While you have your horizontal rope to work on, you might as well go for the Rolling Hitch now (see Fig 37). It is useful when hitching up to a mooring line, or for hanging your trousers to dry in the rigging. It is similar to the Clove Hitch, but has an extra turn.

## Method

Take a clockwise turn (viewed from the right) around your static line.

Take another turn to the left of the first, but *include the standing part* in the turn (see Fig 38).

Now make a third turn to the left of the standing part and tuck the end through (see Fig 39).

Snug up the knot and take the strain on the standing part, near parallel to the static line.

As you can see, the knot does not slide when tension is applied. If you tie a rope in this way on to its own standing part, it forms a loop which is adjustable, but be sure to make it the right way up or the loop will close up.

The Rolling Hitch is a useful knot to know when you have riding turns on a winch – attach another line to the jammed sheet using this hitch and take the load on another winch, so freeing off the sheet.

There is a second way of forming this Hitch for use on a smooth, hard surface, such as a pole or spar. In this case the second turn is taken to the right of the first, then hitched as before (see Fig 40).

It takes a few goes to realize that it is exactly the same knot, and that you can make one from the other just by re-arranging the first two turns. But do not use either form to moor up to a vertical post if the tide is falling, or you may start a new trend in hanging dinghies.

# Buntline Hitch

There is one more Hitch you may find useful, and that's the Buntline Hitch (see Fig 41). It is usually made through an eye or a ring, and is in fact a Clove Hitch made on its own standing part, with the second turn on the inside of the loop so that it jams against the eye when pulled up. It can be used to begin a seizing.

# Figure of Eight

When you are steaming (figuratively speaking) up the Channel in a force seven south-westerly, sails billowing, sheets

Fig 41   Buntline Hitch.

33

Fig 42    Figure of Eight.

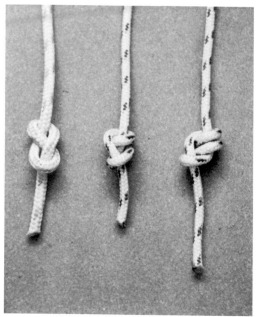

Fig 43    Left to right: Figure of Eight; Stopper Knot; Stevedore Knot.

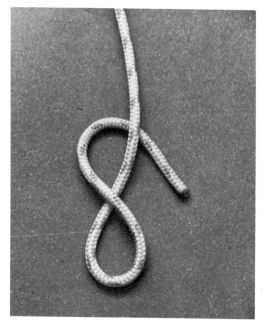

Fig 44    Across the front and round the back.

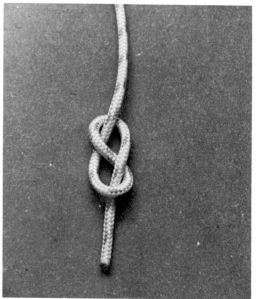

Fig 45    Poke end down through loop.

straining and crew heaving, you will be jolly glad you learned to tie a Figure of Eight (*see* Fig 42) to stop those sheets disappearing through their blocks and fairleads. There's nothing more irritating than having to retrieve the mainsheet end and reeve it through the multiple purchase block on the end of a thrashing boom whilst under considerable way. The Figure of Eight is bulky enough to stop at most eyes, but you can always add an extra turn or more before tucking the end through. It then becomes a Stopper Knot, or even a Stevedore Knot (*see* Fig 43).

## Method

This is easily understood by referring to the diagrams, but for those who just revel in written instructions – allow about 30cm of free rope end for practising (you will soon learn how close to the end to begin, depending on the thickness of the rope you are using). Take the end across the front of the standing part, then round and across the back (*see* Fig 44).

Bring the end forward and poke it down through the loop (*see* Fig 45). It doesn't matter whether you start with the end crossing to left or right – you end up with the same basic knot.

Use it on the ends of all your running rigging, as well as the main and jib sheets, unless you are racing, when it becomes imperative that your crew run up and down the side decks, feeding the genoa sheets through different blocks, for optimum performance and maximum crew-cred.

## Reef Knot

During this same, rather blowy Channel passage, you may also have call to use those little bits of twine dangling in neat rows across the mainsail – the reef points, by which the sail area can be reduced. This is the most obvious use of the Reef Knot, but it can be utilized in various situations, such as tying your flaked mainsail to the boom, keeping oars together, tying your French sticks into bundles, in fact many situations call for using short lengths of rope with the ends tied together around something. Just remember – right over left, left over right, and you can't go wrong.

## Method

Take an end in each hand. Cross the right end over the left end, tuck it around and through, making a half knot, as when you tie your shoelaces (*see* Fig 46).

Now take the left end over the right, around and through, making another half knot on top of the first (*see* Fig 47). This is a Reef Knot, and both ends should be on the same side of their respective standing parts.

*Never* use this knot to join two ropes together, as a bend. Why? Take one of the ends in one hand and its adjacent standing part in the other. Give them a sharp tug in opposite directions. You now have a situation where the knot is said to have 'capsized' (*see* Fig 48) and in this case the ropes will part company by one slipping through the other. That is why you never use a reef knot as a bend. (But it is a quick and easy way of untying it.)

A note here about Reef Knots in small or slippery rope: put in an extra tuck when making both parts and you have the Surgeon's Knot (*see* Fig 49). If it's good enough for sutures, it's good enough for sail ties.

Fig 46    Right over left.

Fig 47    Left over right.

Fig 48   A 'capsized' Reef Knot.

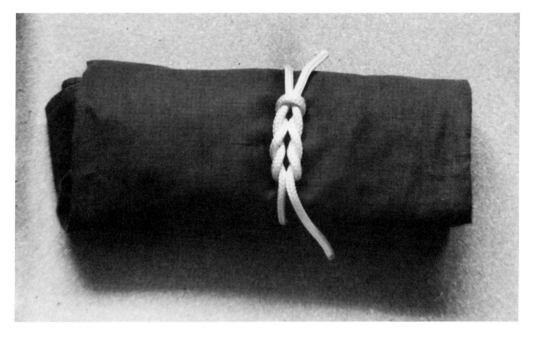

Fig 49   Surgeon's Knot.

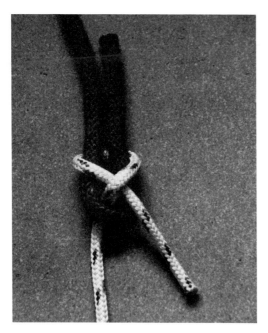

Fig 50   Sheet Bend.

## Sheet Bend

If you do need to join two ropes together, and you don't have sufficient length of rope to make two bowlines, the Sheet Bend (*see* Fig 50) is quick and easy. You can use it to join ropes of equal or unequal diameter. Where applicable, the bight is made in the larger of the two.

### Method

Make a loop near the end of one rope, short end on the right. Pass the end of the other rope up through the loop, around the back from right to left, and tuck through its own standing part, but not through the loop (*see* Fig 51).

This is fine for attaching courtesy flags to their halyards, but for any other purpose use the Double Sheet Bend (*see* Fig 52),

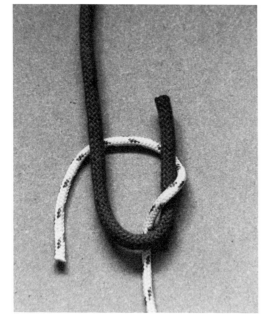

Fig 51   Tuck through standing part.

Fig 52   Double Sheet Bend.

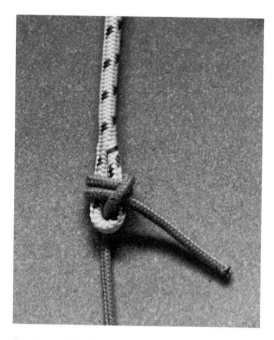

Fig 53    Double Becket Bend.

all can be seized for greater security, especially on ropes of differing thickness.

## Constrictor Knot

There is a very useful knot which could be included in many sections of this book. The Constrictor Knot (*see* Fig 54) can be used to good effect whilst splicing, whipping, decorative knotting, and around the boat in general where there is a need for a binding knot which will not slip. It can be used on standing rigging if you apply some tape first. In some instances it can only be removed by cutting, so be very careful where you use it! It is similar to a clove hitch, but the ends cross each other, forming a half knot with a crossing turn.

which is more secure, especially on modern ropes which may be slippery, and also where there is considerable difference in the thickness of the two ropes. It is also easier to untie than the single.

For the double, just add an extra turn through the tuck. In both knots, do make sure that the ends of both ropes finish on the same side of the knot. If they do not, you have what is known as a left-handed Sheet Bend, which is in fact a weaver's knot.

A welcome note here is that now you have mastered the Sheet Bend and Double Sheet Bend, you are also automatically *au fait* with the Becket Bend and Double Becket Bend. These are identical, but the different names denote that they are tied through a closed eye, or becket, rather than through an open loop (*see* Fig 53). All four knots are better under tension, and

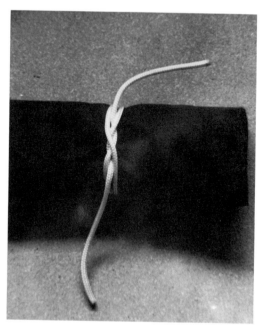

Fig 54    The Constrictor.

Fig 55   Don't make a Clove Hitch . . .

Fig 56   . . . put the end under the 'cross'.

## Method

With the end on the right, make a turn. Make another turn to the left of the standing part, as if you were making a Clove Hitch (*see* Fig 55). Now, instead of tucking the end under diagonally, parallel with the turn already caught, *pass it under the 'cross'* vertically, in a direction away from you. (Not horizontally from left to right or right to left.) Make sure it is under both turns (*see* Fig 56).

Practise making this knot in large-diameter rope so that you can see the structure. It is more fiddly in small stuff, but that is exactly where its forte lies. You will find it invaluable when you come to the decorative knotting section, but it can more usefully be employed to mend broken gear at sea until a permanent repair can be made.

# Lorryman's Hitch

Though not strictly a sailing knot, the Lorryman's Hitch must come under the heading of vital knots. It is also known as the Truck Driver's Hitch and the Waggoner's Hitch.

This hitch is extremely useful for tightening things like lashings, when transporting boats on roofracks or trailers. If you cover your boat in winter with a huge polytarp or a heavy tarpaulin, you can use the Lorryman's Hitch to prevent it puffing in and out like a demented barrage balloon. The action of tightening is known as *bowsing down*.

## Method

You need a solid anchoring point through which to lead the end of the rope which is

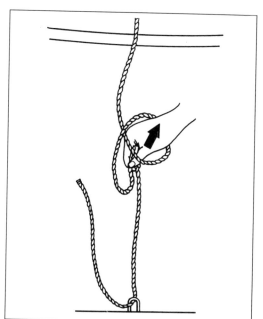

Fig 57　Reach through loop and pull up a bight.

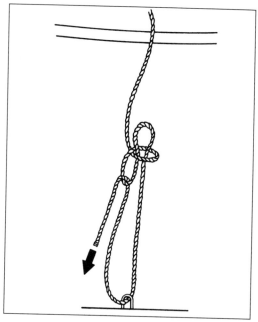

Fig 58　Put end through bottom loop and pull downwards.

attached to whatever you want bowsed down. This could be a strut on a trailer, a purpose-made eye or part of your laying-up cradle.

When you have led the end through, make a loop in the standing part as if you were starting a Bowline. Put your hand down through the loop and bring up a bight from the rope below, the part which has not gone through the anchor point. As you do so, swivel your thumb, which is holding the crossover point, down and around so that it sticks through the small loop made as you bring the bight up through. This little loop, with your thumb in it, is the one through which you put the end of the rope, from the back towards you. When you pull down on the end, the upper loop is gripped by the hitch which makes the lower loop, which in turn is tightened by the hauling down action (*see* Figs 57 and 58).

When the lashing is as tight as required, lead the end back through the anchor point and put on a couple of half hitches around all parts.

---

**SUMMARY**

- Use the correct knot for a given situation.

- If you only learn one knot, make it the Bowline.

- Practise the knots until you can make them in the dark – you may have to.

---

# 6
# EMERGENCY KNOTS

There are several knots which need to be included in this section. They are those which have extremely limited use under normal circumstances but in an emergency they suddenly become compulsory. You can practise them on those long voyages when you have mislaid the playing cards.

## Sheepshank

This knot is recommended for shortening a line temporarily, on the rare occasion that you cannot pull up on one of the ends. The other use is as a sort of Bandaid for chafed rope – you can isolate the worn part in the centre of the shank. It would have to be a dire emergency for any sailor worth his salt to use chafed rope for any

application – always carry copious amounts of spare, whether Atlantic crossing, coastal hopping or jaunts around the buoys.

There is more than one way to make a Sheepshank. This is the easiest to

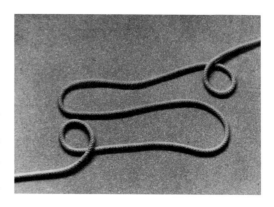

Fig 60   Hitch on each end.

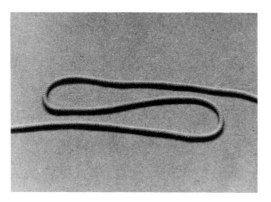

Fig 59   The long 'S'.

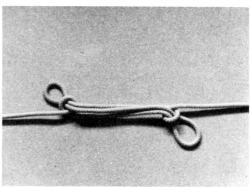

Fig 61   Sheepshank completed.

describe, and your best bet is to make it on the deck. Form the rope into an elongated 'S' shape with the chafed part, if applicable, in the centre of the 'S' (*see* Fig 59). Make a Half Hitch in the line above the right-hand loop and slip it over (the loop). Make a Half Hitch in the line below the left-hand loop, and slip that over (*see* Fig 60). When you apply tension to both ends, you will see that you have two 'ears' sticking up, held by the Half Hitches (*see* Fig 61). These should be seized to the standing parts, because when the tension is released, the whole thing can very easily fall apart. Its redeeming feature is that it can be tied while both ends are attached to something.

## Carrick Bend

In the unlikely event of your having to tie a couple of wire hawsers together, or even very large diameter rope, then the correct way is with a Carrick Bend. This bend forms very rounded bights, hence its use with wire. It is a woven knot, and the instructions are complex, but the diagrams make it clear, provided you make the under/over passes in the correct order.

### Method

Make a clockwise loop in the first rope, end on top. Take the second rope diagonally across the loop and around the back of the standing part of the first rope (*see* Fig 62).

Now the weaving starts: with the second rope go over the first end, under the first standing part, over the second standing part, under the first loop.

You now have two intertwining loops with the ends emerging from opposite

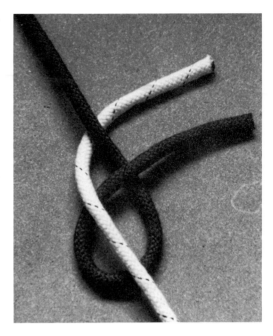

Fig 62   Beginning the Carrick Bend.

Fig 63   Weaving completed.

44

provide a means of stopping it slipping downwards. Study the diagrams carefully, and make sure you pull the right loops in the final move.

## Method

Begin thus: make three clockwise loops, as if you are coiling the rope. Lay them face down and spread them out a little, so they are just overlapping.

The loop on the left should be on top, the loop on the right should be underneath (*see* Fig 65). This gives you three loops with the two outside loops touching in the centre.

Take the two touching parts and overlap the right part over the left part, without disturbing the rest of the loops (*see* Fig 66).

Now for the tricky bit – pass your *left* hand over, then under the two left-hand loops (over first, under second) and grasp the third loop. *At the same time*, pass your right hand under, then over the right-hand loops, and grasp the third loop (*see* Fig 67).

When you carefully pull outwards with both hands, the centre loops weave through the outer loops and form two 'ears' (*see* Fig 68). Pull up (away from you) the centre loop lying at the top, and you have made three complete loops (*see* Fig 69).

In fact, if you grasp the centre loop in your teeth, at the same time as pulling sideways with your hands, the knot forms more evenly. If you have used a short length of rope, you can seize the ends to the side loops, and attach stays to all three loops using Becket Bends. If you have used a long line, you can use these ends for extra staying. I am sure that if you find yourself needing to use the Jury Knot in its

Fig 64   Carrick Bend under tension.

sides of the knot (*see* Fig 63). Pull the knot up neatly. This is a Carrick Bend before tension is applied.

When you pull the ends hard it will distort into something unrecognizable from your neat, symmetrical weaving (*see* Fig 64). A word of caution – if you use this bend in small stuff and it is subjected to much tension, be prepared to untie it using the *knife method*!

## Jury Knot

Let's hope you never need this one, but the Jury Knot is the right one to use if you suffer a broken mast. It slips over the top of the mast (or whatever you have left of it) and the loops are used to secure stays and shrouds, tensioning the central part around the masthead, though it is advisable to

Fig 65    Loops laid down.

Fig 66    Overlap right over left.

Fig 67    Grasping the loops.

Fig 68    Pull outwards.

Fig 69   Pull top loop upwards.

proper context, you will have no trouble finding a use for the ends!

Incidentally, this knot can be used also around the bottom of a jury mast as a way of keeping it central, assuming it has been sliced off at deck level, and there is no way of stepping the jury rig.

---

**SUMMARY**

- These are purpose-specific knots.

- Do not ignore them in the hope that you won't need them.

---

# 7
# WHIPPING

When you are sitting in the cockpit wondering where you picked up the assortment of well-used shaving brushes adorning the ends of your ropes, it is time to consider finishing them off properly, and to my mind, you can't beat a good whipping. It is quick, neat, and leaves the rope more or less the same diameter right to the end, unlike a backsplice.

There are plain whippings and there are fancy whippings, tied whippings and sewn whippings. The thread used can be polyester or nylon, available by the reel in different colours and thicknesses. Waxed twine is easier to use; and you can wax your own using a block of beeswax. If you are working with natural fibre, and the work is of a decorative nature, you can either make your own twine by stranding whatever you are using and waxing it, or alternatively use one of the darker synthetic twines.

Traditionally, the width of whipping is approximately equal to the rope diameter, and it is worked towards the end of the rope.

## Common Whipping

As a means of finishing an end, Common Whipping is no more than adequate, but it is easily mastered.

Take some three-strand rope and a half-metre (18in) length of whipping twine. Fold the end of the twine and place it on

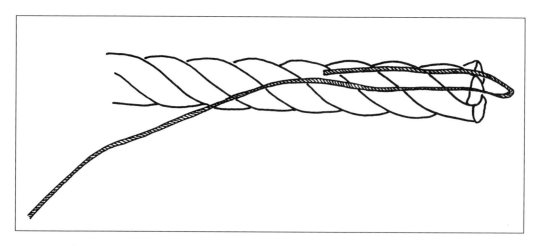

Fig 70  Fold twine and place on rope.

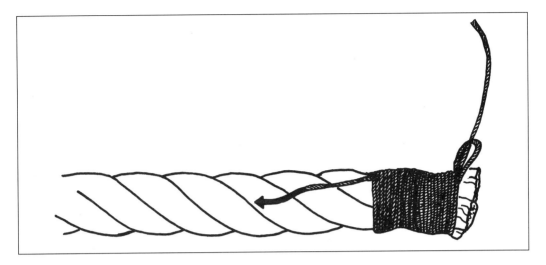

Fig 71    End goes through loop.

the rope, as pictured (*see* Fig 70). Make enough turns with the twine to give you the right length of whipping, then pass the end of the twine through the loop (*see* Fig 71). Pull the other end of the twine which forms the loop, and hey presto, the end disappears under the turns. Don't pull too hard or it will come right out again. The idea is to pull the loop into the centre of the whipping, then cut off both ends (*see* Fig 72).

The biggest problem with this whipping is that if one turn is damaged, the whole thing will unwind and fall off.

Fig 72    Finished whipping.

## West Country Whipping

This avoids losing the whipping through damage to one turn. Start with a cut length of twine, say about 30cm (12in), and put the rope between your knees, end protruding upwards. Centre the twine around the rope and tie a half knot. Take both ends of the twine around to the other side and tie another half knot. Carry on in this way until the required number of turns is completed, and keep all the half knots the same way up for neatness. The final knot should be a Reef Knot, or a Surgeon's Knot (Reef with extra tucks). As you can see, if one strand is worn or cut, the knots will hold the other turns until you can make a proper repair – but do not leave it too long (see Fig 73).

Fig 73   West Country Whipping – a series of Half Knots.

## Sailmaker's Whipping

This has a sewn appearance but is made without the aid of tools, and is more secure than the previous two types.

The starting point is with the rope unlaid for a few turns. Make a loop in the whipping twine and put it over one strand with the ends emerging between the other two strands, and the loop being left long (see Fig 74). Lay up the rope again, giving each strand a slight twist with its own lay to ensure proper bedding. Make the required number of turns with the whipping twine, making sure you leave the loop and the end free (see Fig 75). Drop the loop over its own strand and pull the short end to tighten (see Fig 76). Take this end up to the top of the whipping and tie a Reef Knot with the two ends, so that it lodges in the centre of the rope. Ensure all turns and ends are pulled tightly into place. Trim end, or heat seal synthetics (see Fig 77).

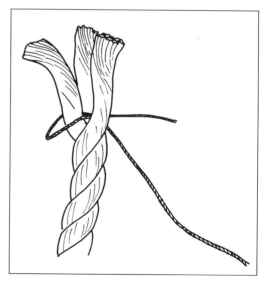

Fig 74   Ends emerge between two strands.

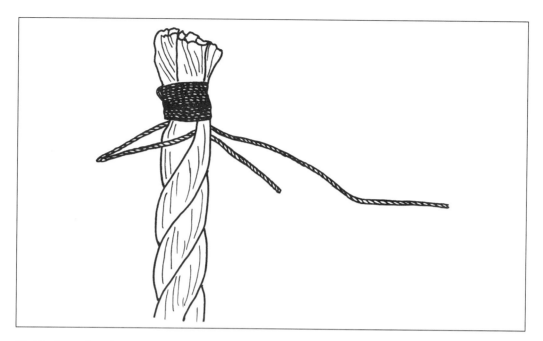

Fig 75   Leave loop long.

Fig 76   Drop loop over its strand.

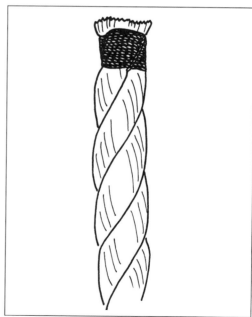

Fig 77   Finished Sailmaker's Whipping.

# Palm and Needle Whipping

This is another type of whipping; it does require the use of tools and is more time consuming, but it is infinitely preferable as far as durability is concerned. It is also more attractive and professional in appearance, somewhat like the sailmaker's whipping.

As the name implies, it is sewn, usually with doubled twine, which is quicker in the long run, though you must make sure the strands lie side by side on the turns. Using a leather palm is easily mastered – the action is always away from the body as the needle, is pushed through (*see* Fig 78). If you find your grip slipping on the needle, use a pair of pliers with some tape

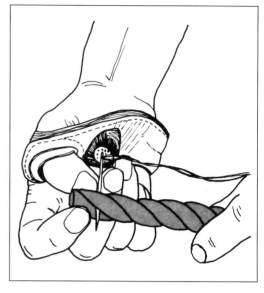

Fig 78   Palm in use.

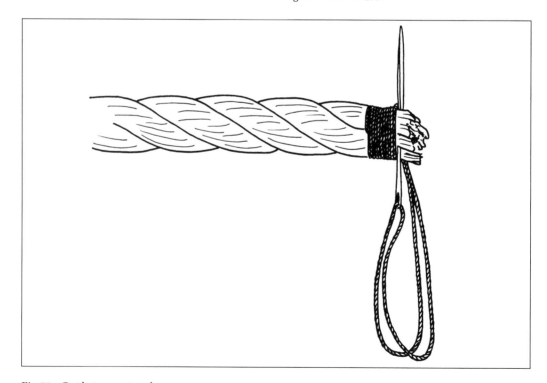

Fig 79   Out between strands.

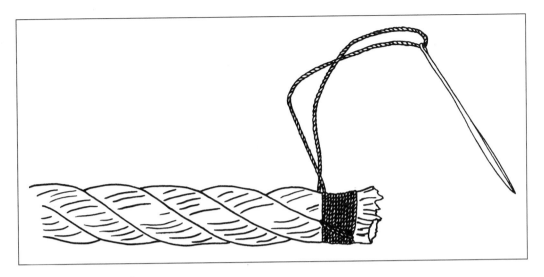

Fig 80   Commence snaking.

on the jaws so you don't rough up the surface of the needle.

So, take a length of waxed twine, thread your needle (preferably a sailmaker's needle but you can get by with a strong common sewing needle) and knot the two ends together. Make a stitch through one of the strands to anchor the end. Make turns around the rope (always work towards the end of the rope) drawing them taut as you go and ensuring they lie flat.

When you have made a suitable number of turns, push the needle through a rope strand and out between the opposite two (see Fig 79). Now, follow the lay of the rope to the other end of the whipping and push the needle through again so that it emerges between the next two strands (see Fig 80). Follow the lay as before to the other end of the whipping, needle in, out between two strands, and so on until you have three diagonal passes over the whipping. (These passes are known as 'snaking'.) Finish by sewing through one strand a couple of times, and trim the end (see Fig 81).

Fig 81   Finished Palm and Needle Whipping.

Palm and needle whipping can also be used on braided rope. The snaking can be increased to good effect on large diameter rope, and you can use both diagonals, resulting in a zig-zag effect (*see* Fig 82).

# French Whipping

This is a type of whipping which is often used to decorative effect as well as for practical purposes (*see* Fig 83). It merely consists of a series of Half Hitches. If you do use it on rope, make sure the hitches follow the lay.

There are other whippings to be found, mainly of a decorative nature, but those I have covered should suffice for all practical purposes.

Fig 82   Different forms of snaking.

---

**SUMMARY**

- Any whipping is better than none, but a sewn whipping is the most durable.

- Use waxed twine for ease.

---

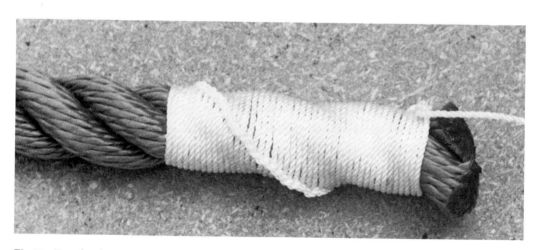

Fig 83   French Whipping.

# 8

# SEIZING

Seizing is very much like whipping, but whereas whipping is used around the strands of one rope to stop it fraying, seizing binds two ropes or two parts of the same rope together, as when forming an eye or securing a knot, such as an Anchor Bend. A waxed whipping twine is usually adequate on a small seizing, but on large ropes choose a synthetic cord of suitable diameter. Considerable tension must be applied on each turn, if necessary using a marline spike.

## The Traditional Way

It is customary to begin by forming an eye in the seizing twine, which can be done by making a Bowline or a Buntline Hitch. The latter has the advantage of tightening on itself, making a more secure beginning to the seizing. The end of the twine is then led around the ropes and through the eye, if applicable, and pulled good and taut (*see* Fig 84).

Fig 84   Starting with a Buntline Hitch.

Fig 85    First layer of turns.

Fig 86    Laying on the riders.

## Method

Take a number of turns, nine or ten, hauling taut each time, and make the last turn a Half Hitch. If you finished it off at this point you would have a Flat Seizing (*see* Fig 85) but this is rather lightweight. A better binding is the Round Seizing, which adds another layer of turns. Do not pull them so hard or they will disappear between the turns on the first layer. This top layer of turns is called *riding turns* or *riders* and always consist of one less turn than the first layer (otherwise the end one would fall off); *see* Fig 86.

The finishing touch is to add some *frapping turns*. These are made at right angles to and around the centre of the seizing turns. Take the end of the twine between the two ropes, bring it up through the centre at the other end of the seizing and make two or three turns, hauling taut.

Fig 87    Fancy frapping turns.

Finishing off can be as interesting as you like to make it (*see* Fig 87). You can make the frapping turns into a Clove Hitch and finish with an overhand knot close up to the turns. You could make a series of Half Hitches around the frapping turns and lose the end in the turns or make a couple of Half Hitches around one of the ropes seized and lose the end in the lay.

All these finishing sequences depend on the thickness of the twine you are using to make the seizing. You would be hard put to make an overhand knot hold in fine nylon, but it would be adequate in a three-strand natural fibre cord around a larger diameter rope.

# Racking Seizing

This is one more seizing which you may find useful as it can stand more strain than a Round Seizing. You can use it to join two ropes if you do not have enough length to knot them, and it is particularly good for putting eyes in braided rope where a splice is not feasible.

## Method

The starting technique is the same as for Round Seizing, then the twine is wound in a Figure of Eight around the two parts which are being seized. On the return layer, which is laid on as for the Round Seizing, the riders bed in between the turns of the first layer, unless the twine is very thin. Finish as for Round Seizing, not forgetting the frapping turns (*see* Fig 88).

## The Easy Way

Leave a long end and wrap the twine

Fig 88   Racking Seizing in progress.

Fig 89   The Easy Way, with Half Hitches.

around as for a Round Seizing, i.e. a layer of turns and a layer of riders. Make frapping turns with the two ends and then tie them together with the knot nestling between the parts of the rope, or make Half Hitches on to the frapping turns with each end. This is a very quick method, but you must still haul taut on the turns (*see* Fig 89).

**SUMMARY**

- Very useful for making eyes in braided rope.

- The first layer of turns *must* be hauled taut.

- Use the *easy way* when time is short.

# 9
# Splicing with Three-strand

Splicing is an extremely useful skill to master. It means you can put eyes in the ends of your mooring ropes instead of Bowlines (or less savoury knots), repair damaged rope, make lines longer and finish off straggly ends.

The strength of a splice depends upon the skill with which it is made, but once the principles are understood, there is nothing to stop you making perfect splices every time.

You will need some lengths of three-strand rope, either synthetic or of natural fibre, about 9mm in diameter (not too fiddly and not too gross). If you are using synthetic-fibre rope, then you will need a heat source for sealing the ends of the strands. Natural fibre can be taped. A marline spike may be necessary also.

## Before You Start

A word about using spikes and fids: when you are using either of these tools to make spaces between the strands, make sure the point is pushed *away* from you and *do not* rest the work directly on your lap. A puncture wound from a marline spike which has just been used to undo a rusty shackle is really not to be recommended.

It is not always necessary to use a spike – some rope is soft enough to enable you to work with your hands only. This is something you will learn by experience. Practise with and without tools – you may not always be in a position to choose.

There is only one term to remember. A *tuck* is where you take a strand over an adjacent strand and thread it under the next strand. This is 'making a tuck' and when you have done this with all three strands, you have made a 'round of tucks' or 'one full tuck'.

## Eye Splice

We are going to start with this one which is probably the most useful of all. My first Eye Splice was a nightmare – I kept getting the third tuck wrong because I wasn't doubling it back. You will see what I mean. It is important to follow the diagrams carefully and endeavour to get it right from the first tuck. It is that third strand which can cause problems and it is important to turn the whole eye over to see what you are doing, or you will tuck it under the wrong strand. Another thing to remember, particularly pertinent to the eye splice, is that the tension must be equal on *all three strands*. There is no point in making a splice which hangs on

59

Fig 90   How not to do it – there was a 12-metre boat (40-footer) on the end of this!

Fig 91   Tape the ends.

one strand (*see* Fig 90). The way to even the tension is by pulling on the eye after each round of tucks until each strand carries the same load, but not quite pulling the strands out of their tucks.

The first thing you need to do is unlay the rope. The length for which you unlay it depends upon the diameter of the rope and the type of splice you are making. There are arbitrary rules ranging from a particular number of rope diameters to 'one turn for every tuck', but experience is the best measure, and the more splices you make, the better will become your judgement. (Better to unlay too much than not enough, of course!)

In this instance, with your 9mm diameter rope, unlay for about 8cm (3½in)

and stop it unlaying any further by taping it or putting on a Constrictor Knot. Seal or tape the ends of the three strands to make tucking easier. Loop the rope around to form an eye, and arrange the strands as pictured (*see* Fig 91). Start with the centre strand and tuck it under one strand of the standing part against the lay (*see* Fig 92). Endeavour to maintain the correct twist in the strands when they have been tucked. Take the strand which is towards the inside of the loop and tuck it under the next strand round at the same level (*see* Fig 93). Now turn the whole thing over and tuck the remaining strand under the remaining standing strand. This is the only one at the same level which does not already have a strand under it. Make sure you make the tuck in the same direction, *against the lay*, which may seem awkward at first as there is a tendency to want to tuck it the wrong way (*see* Fig 94).

If all has gone well, that's the first round of tucks completed. Even up the tension,

Fig 92    Start with centre strand.

Fig 93    Inside strand next.

then make another round of tucks in this way: take a working strand over its adjacent standing strand, and tuck it under the next standing strand. Do the same with the remaining two strands. You can see that the action is a weaving one, over, under, over, under, and that one round must be completed before you begin the next.

Fig 94    Turn it over and tuck 'back'.

Fig 95    Nearly finished.

The number of tucks is also a bit arbitrary, though it has more to do with how soft and slippery the rope is than anything else. I would make three full tucks in a natural fibre, and five in polyester or nylon. Polypropylene, being of a particularly stiff but slippery nature, merits six or seven rounds (*see* Fig 95).

When you have made the required number of full tucks, remove the stopping and finish the ends. The easiest way with synthetic rope is to heat seal each strand close to the rope, but be careful not to melt anything but the ends. With natural fibre, just cut off the ends close to the rope.

## Short Splice

If you need a rope which is longer than any you possess, then the obvious thing to do is knot a couple together. This is fine as a temporary measure, but for a permanent solution you could splice them, using the Short Splice. Just remember you will be left with a join which probably will not go through a block.

Take two lengths of rope and unlay one end of each for about 8cm (3½in). You need to make the strands of one rope intertwine with the strands of the other, so that they alternate (*see* Fig 96). Until you become more experienced at short splicing, you can tape or tie the three strands of one rope to the standing part of the other. This is called stopping, noun and verb. Now take a working strand and pass it over the adjacent strand in the other (non-working) rope, then under the strand next to that (*see* Fig 97). Do the same thing with the other two strands, one at a time. You will not have the same problem as with the Eye Splice, because the direction is clear. Make three full tucks. Remove the

Fig 96   Intertwine ropes and put on a stopping.

Fig 97   First tuck.

Fig 98   Completed Short Splice.

stopping and repeat the process with the remaining three strands. Remember to follow the rules regarding tension. Finish the strands, and that's the Short Splice (*see* Fig 98).

## Backsplice

If you find that the lines on your bucket ropes and fenders are getting shorter and shorter as you keep cutting off the frayed ends, then it's time to start thinking about giving them a Backsplice. There are, of course, easier ways of finishing a rope end. If it is synthetic you can heat seal it. If it's natural fibre you can whip it. If you are lazy you can wrap it in electrical tape or tie a knot in it. But there is no substitute for a neat Backsplice.

First, unlay the rope for about 8cm (3½in), and put on a Crown Knot to stop it unlaying any further, as follows. Hold the rope in your hand with the end sticking upwards, the strands splayed out as in the diagram, noting the way the ends are numbered (*see* Fig 99). Curve 1 around to cross 2, leaving a loop (*see* Fig 100). Hold

end 1 down and lead end 2 away from you and hold down to the left of 3 (*see* Fig 101). Cross 3 over the centre of the knot and tuck down through the loop left in 1 (*see* Fig 102). Pull ends to even the tension. The Crown Knot is now completed. You will see that this is made in the same direction as the lay (I am assuming you have not tracked down some obscure rope with left-handed lay on which to practise) and the ends are pointing back along the rope. If you try it against the lay, you will find that it does not stop the rope unlaying but actually encourages it to do so.

To continue the Backsplice, take an end and tuck it under itself, just below the Crown Knot. You can make sure it is through 'itself' by following the strand back through the knot as a check. Repeat with the two remaining strands (*see* Fig 103). Make more rounds of tucks. It is of absolutely no consequence how many full tucks you make. This is purely a finishing device, though it can serve to remind you that the end of the rope is about to slip through your fingers unless you are very quick (*see* Fig 104). Again, a rope with a backspliced end is difficult if not

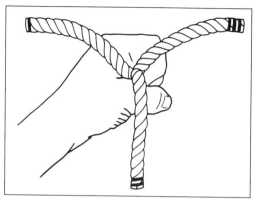

Fig 99   Splay the ends out.

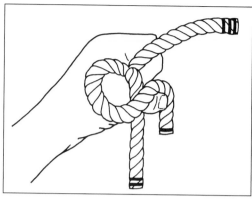

Fig 100   1 over 2, leaving loop.

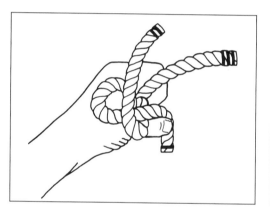

Fig 101   Lead 2 away and hold down.

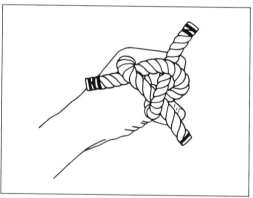

Fig 102   3 over centre and tuck through loop.

Fig 103   Tuck strand through itself.

Fig 104   Finished splice.

impossible to reeve through a block or sheave, so it's back to the Whipping if necessary.

## Tapering Splices

As a way of finishing, splices can be tapered, which entails cutting out half the thickness of each strand, tucking one round, then removing half the thickness of what is left and making a final tuck (*see* Fig 105). This is attractive to look at and adds to the strength of the splice under load, but it is not commonly seen. Another infrequently used finish is to cross-whip the ends after the last tuck (*see* Fig 106), sometimes erroneously called 'dogging'. Divide each strand into two bundles and whip together the adjacent halves. This is particularly secure, especially on large diameter rope, as it is impossible for the tucks to pull out.

Fig 105   Tapered splice.

Fig 106   Cross-whipped ends.

### SUMMARY

- Tension is everything.

- Get the first round of tucks right and the rest is easy.

- Cross-whip the ends for greater security.

# 10

# SPLICING BRAIDED ROPE

When I was about eight years old, I attended a magic show given by a schoolfriend. I didn't see many of the tricks because I was too busy fighting with a tube of braided material which she had slipped over my finger right at the beginning of the performance.

No matter how hard I pulled, the tube just became tighter. This was my first encounter with the Chinese Finger Puzzle. If you take a piece of braided rope and remove the core you are left with just that. Put your finger inside and pull. The braid closes up and grips like a vice. To remove your finger, push the braid so that it widens, hold the far end and slide your finger out. Magic.

If you look at the braid you can see how it works. The strands are plaited so that they run in a diagonal formation. When the ends of the braid are pushed towards each other, the braid becomes wider and shorter; when pulled it lengthens and narrows, tightening around anything in the centre (*see* Fig 107).

This principle of gripping is particularly useful when splicing hollow braid rope, but it also contributes to splices in the other types of braided rope, and is particularly pertinent when splicing braid to wire.

There are many different types of braided rope on the market, and more are being added all the time. It is strong, easy on the hands and comes in a vast array of sizes and colours, so you can be sure you will use it on your boat somewhere, possibly almost everywhere.

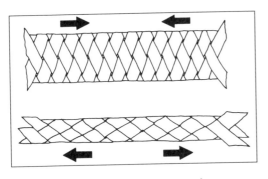

Fig 107   Chinese Finger Puzzle principles.

## Braid on Braid

This is the most common type of braided rope and consequently the one you are most likely to be splicing. The outer sheathing and inner core share any load on the rope, so it is important to ensure that a splice does not upset the balance. (The exception to this is with a rope using a Kevlar core, where the core is the primary load bearer.)

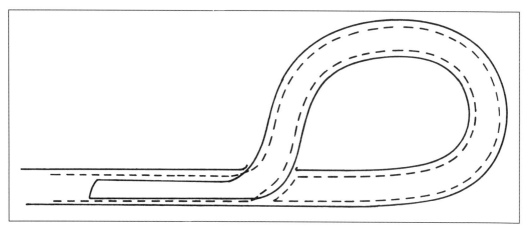

Fig 108   What goes on inside.

## Eye Splice

It is worth gaining an understanding of what is actually happening to the parts of the rope inside the splice. The core and sheathing are separated, and the sheath is looped around and pushed back inside itself and the core. The core is looped in the opposite direction and is threaded through the sheath. It does not go back inside itself but is cut off at the throat of the eye (*see* Fig 108). Of course, all this activity has to go on outside the sheath, and then it is all pulled back inside again, which explains why the instructions are somewhat long-winded.

It is important to make all the marks in the right places. Use a felt-tipped pen, or pieces of tape (which will need to be removed). Various tools are recommended for braid splicing, though some can be improvized for the purposes of practising. The proper tool for a braid-on-braid eye splice is a tubular fid. They are available in different sizes to suit the rope diameter. Stainless steel ones are available but expensive. Plastic ones are adequate for

occasional use. I have made a perfectly serviceable tubular fid from a piece of copper pipe, tapered at one end. I have also improvized with a knitting needle and a lot of sticky tape.

You will notice that the standard unit of measurement is a 'fid length'. This may seem somewhat untechnological, but when you realize that fids come in different lengths for different sizes of rope, and that large rope will need a larger eye than small rope, then it begins to make sense. As an example, a fid for use with 10mm diameter rope is about 25cm (10in) long. They are also marked with a 'short length' (approximately one third of the length) to help with the measurements. Of course, this is of no help when you are using an old knitting needle (*see* Fig 109)!

You will need an absolute minimum of 2.5m (8½ft) of braid-on-braid rope, 10–12mm diameter. A shiny type like Liros is probably the easier to practise with. Follow the instructions step by step and do not rush it. The latter stages of some braid splices require perseverance, and occasionally brute strength!

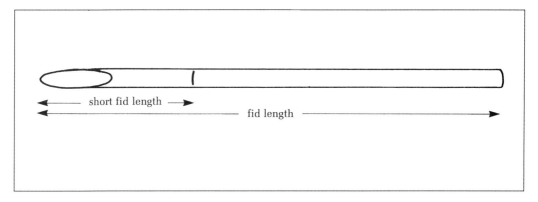

short fid length

fid length

Fig 109   Fid length and short fid length.

## METHOD

1   Tie a good firm Slip Knot in the rope about 2m (6½ft) from the end.

2   Trim off any melted ends, then apply adhesive tape to the end, tightly.

3   Measure a fid length along from the end, and mark a single line right around the sheath. This point will be at the throat of the eye (*see* Fig 110).

4   Form a loop of the required size (if you were inserting a thimble, this would determine the size of the eye, but make a soft eye to begin with) and mark the sheath with a double line at the level of the single line (*see* Fig 111).

5   At the double line, bend the rope sharply and gently prize the strands of the sheath apart and hook a *small* loop of core through with a blunt instrument. Make sure it emerges *between* the plaited strands, not through the middle. Draw a single line around the core where it loops through (*see* Fig 112).

6   Pull out the rest of the core and tape the end tightly.

7   Slide the sheath up towards the knot, effectively extracting more core. It will probably ping back again, so you could apply some tape as a temporary measure to hold it.

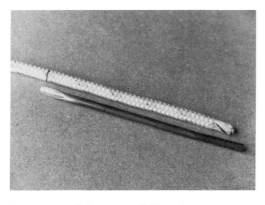

Fig 110   Single line at one fid length.

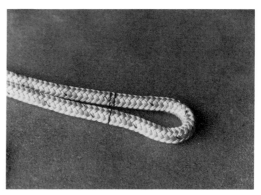

Fig 111   Determine eye size.

Fig 112   Mark core.

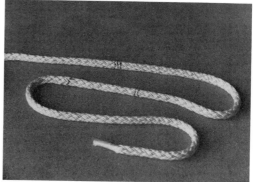

Fig 113   Core with marks 1, 2 and 3.

8   On the *core* mark a double line a short fid length towards the knot, then a triple line one full plus one short fid length up from that. You now have a core with three marks on it (*see* Fig 113).

9   Insert your fid into the core at the double line. Bunch the core onto the fid until it exits at the triple line (*see* Fig 114).

10   Making sure there is no twist in either part, jam the end of the sheath into the end of the fid. You may need to re-tape it and cut it at an angle. You can also extend the tape to make a finer point, and you can use

a layer of tape to hold the sheath in the fid. If you are using a knitting needle, tape the sheath around it as tightly as possible.

11   Holding the core gently, push the fid through the tube, from double line to triple line, until the original single line on the sheath is at the double line on the core. Detach the fid, leaving the sheath tail sticking out of the core (*see* Fig 115). It is at this point that you begin to believe you may actually be able to finish this!

12   Insert fid into the sheath at the original single line, between the strands.

Fig 114   Bunch core onto fid between 2 and 3.

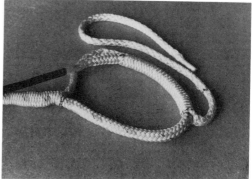

Fig 115   Thread sheath through core until you see single line.

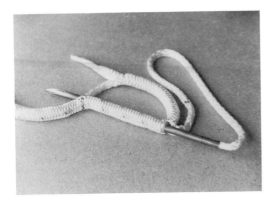

Fig 116   Thread core through sheath from crossover to throat.

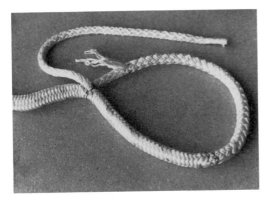

Fig 117   Taper sheath end and smooth core over.

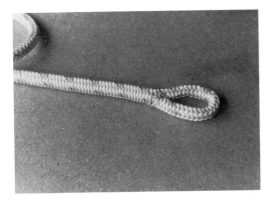

Fig 118   Finished eye before whipping.

This will be the point at which the sheath and the core cross over. Jam the end of the core into the fid, taping again if necessary. The fid now needs to travel around the loop of the sheath to exit at the double line, exactly where the core emerges. This can be accomplished in several stages, by re-inserting the fid exactly where it emerges until you can exit it at the double line (*see* Fig 116). Remember the Chinese Finger Puzzle principle. If the fid seems too tight, *push* the sheath between your hands to make it wider. You now have an eye with two tails. Pull both tails tight so that the crossover point is snug. Remove fid from end of core.

13   Remove any tape from the end of the sheath and unravel the strands back to its exit point. The strands need to be tapered by cutting out bundles at staggered intervals. Divide the bunch into four and cut three of them out at a quarter, half and three-quarters the distance from the exit point respectively. Leave the fourth full length.

14   Hold the crossover point near the top of the eye and smooth both sides of the eye down towards the throat. The tapered ends should disappear inside the core (*see* Fig 117).

15   Now hold the rope at the Slip Knot and gently slide the sheath back towards the eye, using a 'milking' action. The tail of the core is still hanging out (don't worry about it) but the core, with the sheath buried in it, is disappearing into the sheath. It probably will not disappear without a fight, so persevere until the sheath has covered the core completely and there is no slack. It helps if you attach the Slip Knot to a fixed point, enabling you to work with both hands.

16   The core tail can now be cut off about 15mm (⅝in) from its exit point. Pull on the

eye, and the tail should just disappear inside the sheath. If it doesn't, leave it be because it will pull in under load the first time you use it (*see* Fig 118).

17  Put a whipping on the rope, close to the eye.

You have now completed your first Braid on Braid Splice!

## Braid on Braid to Wire

On those yachts which still use wire halyards, a rope tail is reasonably simple to attach, provided the wire is of 7 × 19 or 6 × 19 construction. The rope must be twice the diameter of the wire to ensure that the outer sheath slides over the core splice.

Apart from the usual knife, felt pen, measuring tape, cups of coffee, you will need wire cutters, vinyl tape and a Swedish pattern fid, though you may get away with a spike. I will describe the splice for 7 × 19 wire. If you are using 6 × 19 just ignore any reference to the wire core.

### METHOD

1  Put in a Slip Knot 2m (6½ft) from the rope end, to keep the sheath and core together. Cut off any heat sealing.

2  Push the sheath up to the knot, exposing about 1.5m (5ft) of core. Apply some temporary tape here to stop the sheath shooting back down the core.

3  Cut off 15cm (6in) of core. Do not heat seal.

4  The wire needs to be threaded inside the core for about 75cm (30in). This seems a lot but the strength of this splice is derived from the Chinese Finger Puzzle principle. Measure 75cm (30in) up the core and mark it. Tape the end of the wire well.

5  Thread a tubular fid through the core and out at the mark, bunching up the core on the fid.

6  Put the wire end in the fid and exit it at the marked point. Though not necessary, if you want to be finicky you can taper the wire at this point by cutting out one strand at 15cm (6in) from the end, one at 12.5cm (5in), one at 10cm (4in) and two at 7.5cm (3in). These need taping well at each level (*see* Fig 119).

7  Smooth the core down and allow the wire to slip back slightly so that the end disappears back inside the core completely.

8  Put some tape or a constrictor around the core about 15cm (6in) up from the loose ends. These now have to be spliced to the wire, so unravel them and divide into three bundles. Put tape on the ends, made into points to help with the splicing.

9  You need to make a splice just as when using three-strand, but tucking under and over *two* strands of wire at a time (*see* Fig 120). Use a spike or a Swedish fid, and pull the strands tightly before removing the tool at each tuck. Make three rounds of tucks. Taper the splice by removing one third of the strands in each group, then tucking a fourth round. Repeat the tapering and tuck a fifth round. Cut off the ends close to the wire and melt the ends by *very carefully* passing a flame close to them, or use a heated knife (*see* Fig 121).

10  You now need to replace the sheath, so remove the temporary tape and milk the cover down over the core splice. The secret is to push, not pull.

11  Put a whipping around the sheath where the core splice ends inside.

12  Unravel the ends of the sheath back to the whipping and divide into three equal bundles. Tape the ends (*see* Fig 122).

71

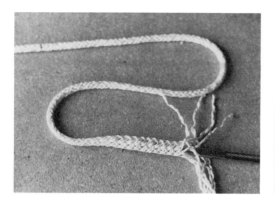

Fig 119  Threading wire up through core.

Fig 120  Under two and over two, ignoring any core wire.

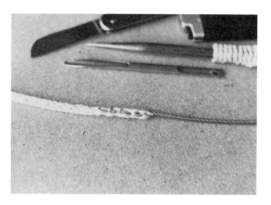

Fig 121  Finished core to wire splice.

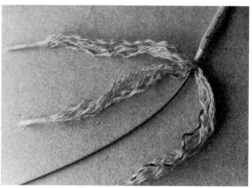

Fig 122  Tape sheath into three bundles.

Fig 123  Bundles spiral around two strands.

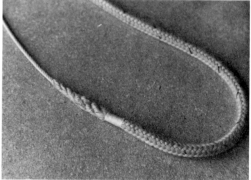

Fig 124  Finished splice.

13   The splice for the sheath is not a conventional over/under splice – the ends travel in the same direction as the lay, rather than opposing it, and the finish is very pleasing. What is actually happening is that each strand is spiralling around the same pair of wire strands.

So, using the spike or fid, lift two wire strands by inserting it against the lay, but tuck a sheath strand (bundle) *towards* you (*see* Fig 123). Repeat with the other two strand bundles around their respective wire strand pairs. The remaining rounds use the same pairs of wire strands for the same sheath bundles. You need to make five rounds, but taper them by removing some yarns on each round.

14   The splice is finished by heat sealing all the ends carefully (*see* Fig 124).

# Braid with Three-strand Core

This type of rope consists of a very strong twisted core of three strands, with a soft and comfortable outer braided sheathing. It requires a slightly different splicing technique as the primary strength is in the core. An example is Marlow 16-plait matt.

## *Eye Splice*

This splice requires the use of a Marlow splicing needle. Bent wire does not work too well during the latter stages as the splice is extremely tight in the sheath. For the same reason, do not attempt it on anything less than 7mm diameter, because there will not be enough space for the splicing tool.

The technique results in the inner core being spliced into an eye inside the sheath, which in turn is threaded down between itself and the core, after being tapered, to emerge at different points along the length of the rope.

It is fairly time consuming and requires considerable force to smooth the sheath over the splice. A very strong fixing point is vital.

METHOD

1   Make a Slip Knot 2.5m (8½ft) from the end.

2   Put a layer of tape on the rope 15cm (6in) from the end and unlay the sheath to this point. Tape the ends of the three core strands separately (*see* Fig 125).

3   Form an eye of the required size and where the tape touches the adjoining part of the rope, make an opening and extract a 25cm (10in) loop of core (*see* Fig 126).

4   Slide back the sheath from the end about 7cm (3in), giving you a total of 22cm (9in) with which to work.

5   Splice the end of the core into the loop, just as you would make a normal three-strand Eye Splice, beginning about 5cm (2in) from where the core emerges. Make four full tucks, then taper the strands and make two more tucks (*see* Fig 127).

6   Cut off the ends of the core (do not heat seal) leaving about 2cm (¾in), and tape them securely to the body of the core (*see* Fig 128).

7   Attach the slip knot to a very solid anchor point, or you could stand on it, and 'milk' the sheath down over the core splice (*see* Figs 129, 130 and 131) until it disappears inside. This takes considerable effort. Remove tape.

8   The next thing is to incorporate the sheath ends using the splicing tool. Push the eye of the tool into the sheath about 15cm (6in) from the eye, and exit it at the throat of the eye, where the core emerges.

Fig 125    Unlay for 15cm (6in) and tape core ends.

Fig 126    Extract 25cm (10in) of core.

Make sure the needle is fed between the sheath and the core, without snagging (*see* Fig 132).

9    Thread some of the unravelled strands through the tool eye and pull them through until they exit through the sheath.

10    Repeat with the remaining strands, as many times as is necessary to incorporate them all. This will depend on the size of the rope. Stagger the positions at which you insert the tool so that the ends emerge at different lengths from the throat, and on different sides of the rope (*see* Fig 133). If you have trouble threading the tool up to the throat, try making more space by inserting the tool from the throat downwards and wiggling it around, then insert it in the correct manner and pull the strands through where you have, hopefully, made space.

11    Cut off the strands and smooth the sheath downwards (not an easy task) which should make the loose ends disappear (*see* Fig 134). If you have difficulty in achieving points 7 through 10, try using washing-up liquid.

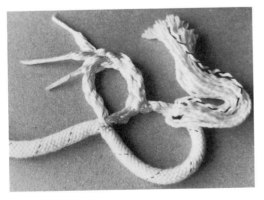

Fig 127    Make a Three-Strand Eye Splice.

Fig 128    Tape ends tightly to the core.

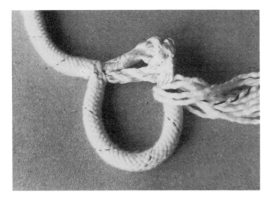

Fig 129   Going . . .

Fig 130   . . . going . . .

Fig 131   . . . gone.

Fig 132   Tool emerging to take sheath ends.

Fig 133   Stagger the exit points.

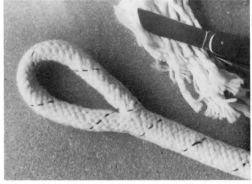

Fig 134   Finished Soft Eye.

Fig 135   Depositing wire into three-strand core.

## Braid with Three-strand Core to Wire

This is so similar to the Braid on Braid to Wire that I am not going to repeat it all. The only difference is in the way the wire is 'wound' into the centre of the core. Follow directions for the Braid on Braid to Wire Splice, numbers 1 through 4. Now position the end of the wire 75cm (30in) from the end of the inner core. Open up the lay of the core at this point and proceed to spiral the core and the wire together, depositing the wire into the centre of the core (see Fig 135). You may find it helpful to put tape around the core and wire at the 75cm (30in) mark. When you reach the end of the core, proceed as for Braid on Braid from number 8, using the three strands as you would the three-core bundles.

## Quick Eye Splice

This is an easier splice and is purported to retain 95 per cent of the rope's strength if correctly done. It can be used on braided rope with three-strand core and with multifilament core.

You will need a Marlow splicing needle or your wire equivalent.

METHOD

1   The first thing is to loosen up the sheath over the core, so cut off any heat-sealing and push the sheath up about 10cm (4in). Hold the sheath and core together at this point and 'milk' the slack up the rope for about 1 metre (3⅓ft).

2   Measure 30cm (12in) from the end of the sheath and mark a single line. This will be the throat of the eye (see Fig 136).

3   Make the eye the size you require and mark a double line level with the single line, then open up the sheath at that point and pull out the core. Lay the two 'tails' parallel and tape the core at a point level with the single line on the sheath (see Fig 137).

4   Insert the splicing tool about 30cm (12in) up the rope from where the core exits. It should travel between the outer sheath and the inner core without snagging, and exit at the single line on the sheath.

5   Taper the core by cutting out half the yarns where they are taped. Thread the end through the eye of the splicing tool (see Fig 138).

6   Pull the tool out, bringing the core with it, and pull it up to close the eye. Feed some of the slack back down towards the eye to give more space for the tool.

7   Unlay the end of the sheath to within 5cm (2in) of the single line, and reduce it by one third, cutting out strands at intervals around the circumference (see Fig 139).

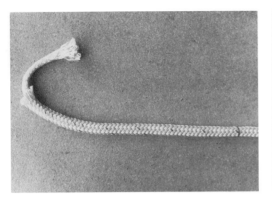

Fig 136    Single line 30cm (12in) up.

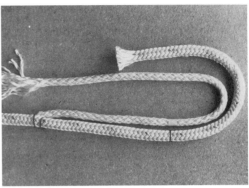

Fig 137    Tape core at single line.

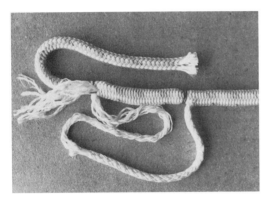

Fig 138    Taper core and thread through tool.

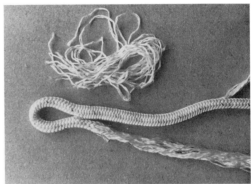

Fig 139    Taper the sheath.

Fig 140    Eye with two tails.

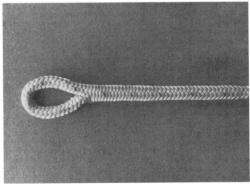

Fig 141    Finished eye.

8 Insert the splicing tool 20cm (8in) down from the throat of the eye, on the opposite side of the rope to that from which the core tail emerges, and exit at the throat. Thread the sheath strands. Extract the tool with the tail of the sheath. You will find that you now have an eye and two tails at intervals down the rope (*see* Fig 140).

9 Make everything tight, giving the eye a firm pull. Cut off the loose ends and smooth the sheath from the eye end until the loose ends have disappeared (*see* Fig 141).

## Eight-Plait Dinghy Eye Splice

Dinghy sheet sizes are chosen for handling comfort, usually 9 or 10mm, offering far greater strength than is necessary. It is adequate, therefore, to use an Eye Splice which requires the removal of a length of core, weakening the rope, but perfectly capable of handling the forces on a dinghy

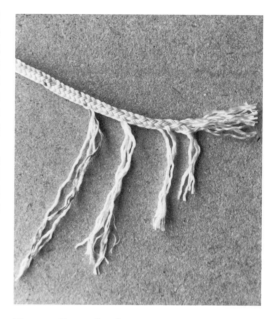

Fig 143   Tapered end.

mainsheet. Do not use this method on keel-boat sheets.

Again, it requires a Marlow splicing needle, a home-made wire substitute, or a double-ended knitting needle and some sticky tape.

METHOD
1   Cut off any heat-sealed ends.
2   Slide sheath back and cut off 70cm (28in) of core. Do not heat seal it.
3   Slide sheath back over the core, firmly. This leaves you with 70cm (28in) of hollow sheath (*see* Fig 142).
4   Taper the end of the sheath thus: cut out a strand at 25mm (1in), 50mm (2in), 75mm (3in) and 100mm (4in), without unravelling (*see* Fig 143).
5   Feel where the core ends and insert the splicing tool or knitting needle about 15mm (⅝in) above the core end, pointing towards the hollow part. Make sure the

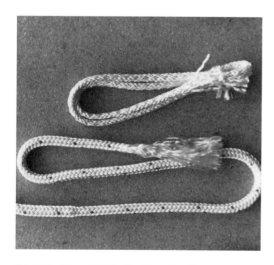

Fig 142   70cm (28in) of hollow sheath.

Fig 144   Braid pulled through.

Fig 145   Trimmed and whipped.

tool feeds between the sheath and core. Exit the eye of the tool, or the point of the knitting needle, 27cm (11in) along the hollow sheath, keeping it on the same side of the rope.

6   Thread the taper into the tool, or tape it to the end of your knitting needle.

7   Extract tool, pulling the tail through to fill the empty braid (*see* Fig 144).

8   Smooth the sheath back towards the eye and adjust until you are happy with the resulting splice. Trim off the raggy ends and give the eye a good tug.

9   As added security, I would put a whipping at the throat of the eye, partly to ensure that the core does not move inside the sheath, but also because, theoretically, it could pull out if you applied the Chinese Finger Puzzle principle (*see* Fig 145).

## Stitch and Whip Eye Splice

This is not a splice at all, but it is a very common way of making an eye in braided ropes. It is a sewn eye with a whipping over the top.

If a thimble is to be used in the eye, it is important for the stitches to pull up tight at the throat.

Use a heavy whipping twine – it takes about 4m (13ft) – and wax it.

METHOD
1   Fold the rope over to form an eye, allowing about 75mm (3in) to sew and whip.

2   Knot the end of the twine and bury it between the two parts by making a stitch close to the eye. Make a double stitch through both parts, and if you are inserting

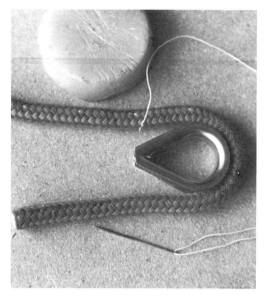

Fig 146   Bury knot between parts.

Fig 147   Work stitches along *and* back.

Fig 148   Finished Whipping.

a thimble, make the stitches as close as possible to the throat (*see* Fig 146).

3   Work a few stitches down to the short end and back, pushing the needle in at an angle and pulling each stitch tight (*see* Fig 147).

4   With the same thread, begin the whipping up close to the eye/thimble and work towards the short end, keeping the twine taut. About half-way along, make a stitch through the standing part as a precaution should the whipping be broken, in which case only half of it would unravel.

5   Carry on to the end and anchor the twine by taking two stitches through the standing part, then stitch along it for about 5cm (2in) and back, before cutting the twine (*see* Fig 148).

It is not necessary to put frapping turns on a whipping of this length, but if you want to do it for appearance, divide the length into three and sew the turns through in three separate lots.

## Multiplait Eye Splice

This rope has eight strands woven in four pairs, two pairs of which have a right-hand lay and two a left. This makes for an interesting appearance, and a construction which gives the rope good handling characteristics as it makes it very supple. It is mostly used for anchor ropes and for mooring. It does not kink.

Some manufacturers, such as Marlow, mark the right-handed pairs with a black thread. Otherwise you may find it useful to mark them yourself until you are familiar with the lay.

Making an Eye Splice is not difficult, provided you do not mix up the strands. Use a diameter of about 16mm for ease of handling, and in practice the eye would be quite large, so use at least a metre (3½ft) of rope, preferably more.

METHOD

1   Allow about 20cm (8in) for the tucking, and put on a whipping at this point.

2   Cut off any heat sealing and unlay the strands back to the whipping.

3   Form an eye in the rope. Tape the end of each pair of strands.

4   Keeping the strands in their pairs, tuck the left-handed pairs under the left-handed pairs on the standing part, and the right-handed under the right-handed (*see* Fig 149).

As for direction, the left ones point to the left and the right ones point to the right as they are tucked. Do a pair of each on the front, then turn over the eye and do the same on the back. Pull snug and even up the tension. This is the first tuck completed. You have tucked four pairs through four double strands on the standing part (*see* Fig 150).

5   Now divide the pairs by removing the tape and tuck singly from now on, under and over, straight along the rope, but one round at a time (*see* Fig 151). Make five full tucks (*see* Fig 152).

6   You can taper the splice by cutting and heat sealing one strand from each pair at this point and making another three tucks with the remaining strands. Alternatively, you can cross-whip the ends, as shown for three-strand splicing. The final picture in the sequence shows a finished splice which has been tapered twice, making a very neat and proper job (*see* Fig 153).

In a mooring rope, the eye is likely to spend a lot of time being placed over bollards, so a length of plastic tubing should be fitted before the splice is begun.

Fig 149　Tuck left under left, right under right, in pairs.

Fig 150　First round completed, rear view.

Fig 151　Divide strands and tuck singly along rope.

Fig 152　Five full tucks made.

Fig 153   The finished Splice, tapered.

## Kevlar and HMPE/Spectra/ Dyneema Core

Due to the fact that virtually all the strength is in the core of these ropes, it is not advisable to stake your life on an amateur splice.

I have a Kevlar splice made by Ian McCormack of XM Yachting which is a work of art, but what goes on inside it is a trade secret, to be discussed at clandestine riggers' meetings. (I have actually dismantled it, not an easy task, and can assure you it is not a splice to be taken lightly.)

The HMPE cores have an added complication in the extra inner sheath, and some manufacturers are still working on splicing techniques for these exotic materials. This is the primary reason for leaving it to the professionals, but another is the not inconsiderable cost of these ropes – a miscalculation during a splice could constitute a very expensive mistake.

## A Final Caution

Splicing braided rope is no easy matter. It is important to maintain the balance of the core and sheath. The tension must be apportioned according to the particular construction; the primary slip knot is to ensure that the core does not slide up inside the sheath while you are working, and upset this balance.

If you have any doubts about the integrity of your braid splices, do not hesitate to leave it to the professional riggers.

---

**SUMMARY**

- Each type of braided rope has a distinct method of splicing.

- Make absolutely sure you are fully conversant with the method before attempting a braid splice.

- If in doubt, leave it to a professional.

---

# 11

# TAKING CARE
# OF YOUR ROPES

Ropes are not cheap, neither are they indestructible. If you want them to last you must treat them with care and respect. It is a common misconception that synthetics are impervious to everything bar a flamethrower, and that they can stay in place for twenty-five years without so much as a fleeting glance.

Waving a bucket of water at them is just not good enough. At the end of the sailing season every sheet, halyard and little dangly bit should be unknotted, unrove and checked centimetre by centimetre for signs of chafe, snagging and ultraviolet degradation. Do this before they are washed – the grime of normal usage often serves to point out the sections needing special attention, such as sheave wear.

If you find such a problem area, ascertain the cause. Is it a sheave which is too small for the rope? Large-diameter rope will not turn happily through tight curves – make sure your sheaves are about five times the diameter of the rope they are carrying, and that the grooves are wide enough to contact a third of the rope circumference. Make sure they all turn freely.

Have you found chafe caused by rough cleats? Smooth with glass paper, or in the case of mast cleats with a fine file.

Halyards and sheets can be turned end-for-end to redistribute the wear and prolong their life, and if your mast is not removed during the off-season, at least replace the halyards with temporary lines which can smack themselves silly against the mast throughout the winter.

A modern-day instrument of rope torture is the line stopper. This acts like a serrated mangle on the poor rope, squeezing it to death in its vice-like grip. A row of stoppers across the cabin top is now the norm, particularly on racing yachts, each with a different-coloured tail emerging from its ravaging jaws. The stoppers are used for halyards and control lines, such as kicking straps. It is worth making them extra long to allow the wear points to be moved periodically. Better to re-splice then re-rig (see Fig 154).

The worst chafe problems are likely to occur on mooring warps. Points to watch are the sections which may contact the toe rail, and those parts which pass through cleats fore and aft. The best way of preventing damage through cleat wear is to use lengths of clear plastic tubing over the salient areas, and the same on large eye splices. This is particularly pertinent on nylon lines, which are very elastic and chafe at the slightest provocation (see Fig 155).

Washing is very important. It removes

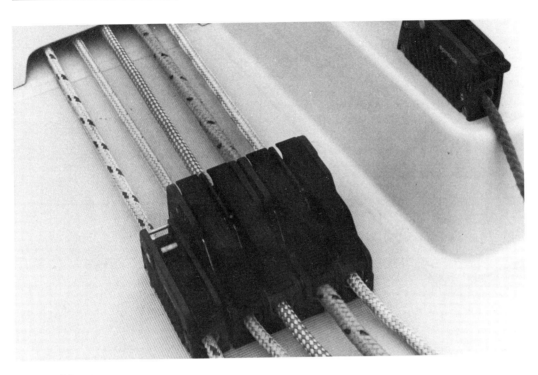

Fig 154   Line stoppers.

Fig 155   The ubiquitous plastic tubing.

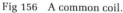

Fig 156    A common coil.

Fig 157    A figure-of-eight coil.

particles of grit, which can wear away at the fibres of the rope, as well as salt which can build up and make the rope stiffer, therefore encouraging more wear. An easy way to wash several ropes together is to put them in a pillowcase or custom-made net bag and put them in the washing machine on a synthetics programme.

According to everything I have read on the subject, it is perfectly OK to store away your synthetic ropes while wet. I cannot for one moment imagine why you would want to do that, especially if your only storage space is the bedroom closet. And if you have ever had the misfortune to smell a shed full of damp rope, you will certainly make sure that yours are dry before you stow them for the winter.

They should be coiled loosely and hanked ready for hanging. This can be done in one of several ways, but first it is important to understand the different characteristics of laid (three-strand) rope and braided rope, when being coiled.

Laid rope (assuming it to be a right-hand lay) is coiled in the normal way: hold rope in left hand with half a metre (1½ft) dangling. Use your right hand to make successive loops which are transferred to the left hand, giving each loop a clockwise (right-handed) twist (*see* Fig 156).

The difference with braided rope is that it has no lay, so the last thing you want to do is introduce twist into it. In this case, make figure-of-eight coils. Repeat the actions as for laid rope, but leave out the

Fig 158   Make a small loop.

Fig 159   End around and through loop.

twist. The coils will automatically form into figures of eight. It may not look as neat as round coils, but it makes for better handling when needed (*see* Fig 157).

If you need to coil laid rope of any great length, say more than 10m (30ft), use the figure-of-eight method, or you will introduce too many kinks for it to be un-coiled satisfactorily.

To make hanks out of the coils, ready for hanging, you need enough rope free at the end for clove hitching onto a locker rail or a hook, so take this into account.

A half hitch coil is common. When you have coiled the rope, make a small loop (*see* Fig 158) and take the end around the top of the coil and back through the loop. Pull tight (*see* Fig 159).

A buntline coil makes a firm 'nipped-in' coil, which is very easy to free off, as there is no end to feed through. Make the coil, common or figure-of-eight, then wrap several turns around near the top of the coil, push a bight of the working end through above the crossing turns and loop it over the top (*see* Fig 160). Take up the slack, and the coil can be hung by the free end which is held in place by the bight. To undo, just lift the bight back over and the end is free to uncoil (*see* 161).

If you have long lengths of large-diameter rope to store, such as anchor warps, coil them in figures of eight on the deck, put stoppings on, fold the two parts of the eight together and tie as one. Store as you would a normal coil.

Fig 160   Push a bight through.

Fig 161   Finished buntline coil.

Ropes containing Kevlar fibre should be made into round coils and stoppings put on at intervals. They can then be suspended by a short length of odd rope which you will find lurking in some dark and inaccessible corner of the cockpit locker.

Some ropes are claimed to be impervious to certain substances, but it is a good idea to keep them all away from oil, grease, tar, battery acid and assorted solvents, as a general rule for rope survival.

**SUMMARY**

- Do not abuse your ropes – wash, dry and store with care, in suitable coils and hanks.

- Check regularly for excessive abrasion.

- Redistribute wear points.

- Keep ropes away from solvents.

# 12

# DECORATIVE KNOTTING

Now we come to the creative part. Decorative knotting is challenging and fun, and what's more you can actually make useful items for your boat, your home, or to give to your immensely impressed friends.

Fancy work comes in various forms, including square knotting, mats, sinnets and knob knots.

Regarding the latter, there are hundreds to be found in knotting books but I have covered just a few of the easier ones here. They look most impressive along the length of a rope, or at the end. They can be of practical use as markers and handholds.

Square knotting is something with which I am very familiar, and I hope you find the small projects stimulating enough to try something of your own design.

Mats are equally functional and decorative, whether preventing the spread of grit or the constant thumping of blocks on the deck.

Sinnets are therapeutic. Making them can be a very relaxed affair – they can be picked up and put down, carried around in your pocket and brought out when you feel the urge to knot. If you carry a short, knobbly key-ring sinnet in your pocket, it serves the same purpose as a string of worry beads!

## Knob Knots

Let's be perverse, and start with the stoppers!

You will need a length of three-strand with which to practise, or preferably several short lengths, as you cannot keep using the same piece. Alternatively, bind together three lengths of braided rope and treat these as strands, the advantage being that you can make and unmake as many knots as you like, and the 'strands' will stay in perfect condition. This method will only work on knots which do not have to be finished by tucking, as in a splice, or re-laying. For clarity in description, I will refer to your rope as if it is three-strand throughout.

The precursor to many of these knots is the Crown Knot which has already been covered in the splicing section (refer to Figs 99–102, page 64). Along with the Crown Knot, you almost always find the Wall Knot, which is very similar, but the strands go 'under and up' instead of 'over and down'. (If you make one of each and turn one upside down, you will see that the actual form is identical. This does not mean they are interchangeable in use!).

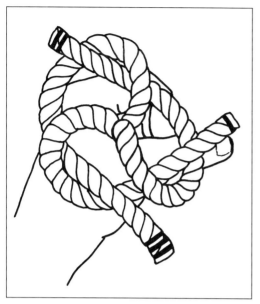

Fig 162   Ends go under and up.

Fig 163   Finished Wall Knot.

## Wall Knot

To make the Wall Knot, take your unlaid rope and hold it as for the Crown Knot. Take end 1 *under* end 2, take 2 under both 1 and 3, take 3 under 2 and through the bight left in 1 (*see* Fig 162). Pull ends firmly. You now have a knot with the ends protruding from the top (*see* Fig 163).

Combine the two knots, Wall first then Crown above it and you have the Wall and Crown – the namesake of many an old English Pub (*see* Fig 164).

## Manrope Knot

A natural progression from the Wall and Crown, which makes a very impressive lump on the end of a lanyard. It is a Wall and Crown Knot doubled, that is to say, the ends are led around both knots a second time. This is where you need to

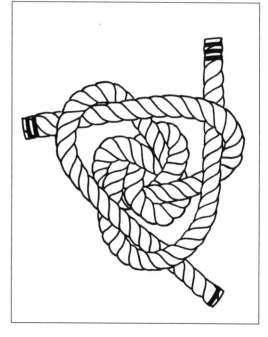

Fig 164   Wall and Crown, view from above.

Fig 165   One end followed through the Wall.

start concentrating and follow some instructions.

Make a Wall Knot, so you have three strands emerging upwards. Make a Crown Knot – three strands pointing downwards. Do not tighten up any part of the knot until the very end – you need the extra space to tuck the ends more than once through the same hole. Now, take any end and follow its own part through the Wall Knot again (*see* Fig 165), then repeat with the two remaining ends, which gives you three ends protruding slightly upwards (*see* Fig 166). Use them to double the Crown Knot, by following their own parts as they tuck under the strands of the existing Crown Knot (*see* Fig 167). Perform the stages methodically, remembering that each action occurs three times (when using three-strand). You should now have a lumpy knot which needs tidying – do not

Fig 166   The Wall doubled.

Fig 167   Follow through the Crown.

Fig 168    Tuck down through and cut off or whip.

Fig 169    Manrope Knot with ends spliced into rope.

just pull the ends, but feed them around, using a spike or small fid if necessary. The ends can be dealt with in several ways, but the easiest is to tuck them down behind the double strands of the Wall Knot so that they emerge alongside the body of the rope (*see* Fig 168). Depending on the type of fibre, they can be cut off close and almost lost in the centre of the knot, or they can be spliced into the lay. The splice can be tapered and whipped for neatness (*see* Fig 169).

Strictly speaking, the Manrope Knot should be made with four-strand material. But if the same moves are followed with each strand, some very impressive knots can be made by increasing the number of strands, either by tracking down some unusual ropes, or by making your own by binding strands together and using a whipped finish.

## Diamond Knot

This is a very easy ornamental knot (*see* Fig 170), but the Double Diamond Knot is much more impressive and looks fine on a lanyard or bell rope. To make the diamond, put a seizing on your three-strand, then turn the unlaid ends back along the length of the rope, and put a temporary stopping on them (*see* Fig 171). Take an end, pass it over the adjacent stopped strand and under the next. Repeat with the other two strands (*see* Fig 172). Remove the stopping and gradually work the knot taut over the seizing. As a single diamond, the ends can be re-laid, then whipped, but better to make a Double Diamond by following the ends round again (*see* Fig 173).

Fig 170   Single Diamond.

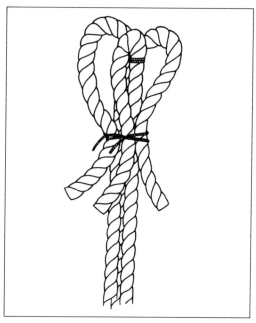

Fig 171   Turn back ends and stop them.

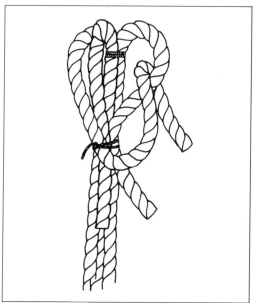

Fig 172   Over one and under next, one end shown.

Fig 173   Double Diamond.

Fig 174   Double Matthew Walker.

## Double Matthew Walker

The section would not be complete without this knot (*see* Fig 174), and here is an incredibly easy way to make it. Begin as with the Diamond Knot, putting a seizing on the rope, turning back the strands and temporarily stopping them. Take any strand and tuck it upwards under the stopped strand next to it (*see* Fig 175). Repeat with the other two strands, working anticlockwise as you look down upon it. If you drew up the knot now it would be a Wall Knot, but you have made one of those already, so take a strand again and tuck it through the adjacent strand, so that it lies alongside the one already there (*see* Fig 176). Repeat with the other strands. If you drew this one up it would be a Matthew Walker. *But*, we are going for the big one, so make one more round of tucks in the same manner, at which point you will see that each strand has made a complete circumnavigation of the rope and tucks through itself (*see* Fig 177). Finally, remove the temporary stopping and draw up the knot carefully and methodically. This is the Double Matthew Walker.

One of the best uses is on bucket lanyards to afford a better grip. Use three-strand rope that you have unlaid, put in the first knot, lay up the rope, put in another, and so on.

A word of advice – when drawing up the knot, don't be afraid to rearrange the strands forming the tucks to make the knot symmetrical. It will not just automatically fall into place. It needs working at. The good thing about this method is that it can be made with any number of strands and tucks, so you can have great fun with it. Experiment with different numbers of strands bound together.

Fig 175  Tuck end through next stopped strand.

Fig 176  Tuck through next stopped strand again.

Fig 177  Each end circumnavigates and tucks through itself.

Fig 178   Left strand up through own bight.

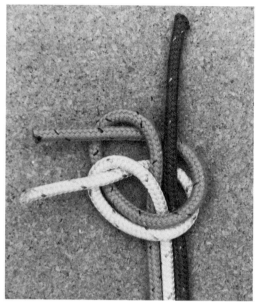

Fig 179   Centre strand in front and up through both bights.

## An alternative Matthew Walker

There is another way of making the Double Matthew Walker which is described in most books of knots. It can be made in the hand with small stuff, but can be more troublesome to draw up neatly. Beginning with the strand on the left, make an overhand knot around all strands, bringing the end up through its own bight (*see* Fig 178). Take the centre strand and do the same, in front of and below the first strand, bringing the end up through both bights (*see* Fig 179). The right-hand strand does the same and comes up through all three bights (*see* Fig 180). Hold the three ends and work the knot into its finished form.

Fig 180   Right strand up through all three bights.

## Double Footrope Knot

Another good stopper, this is nicely rounded and quite hefty (*see* Fig 181). As usual, unlay the strands and make a Crown Knot. Make a Wall Knot below the Crown Knot (*see* Fig 182). Double the Crown Knot by running each end through the knot, parallel to its own part (*see* Fig 183). This gives you three ends pointing downwards. Carry the ends on around the Wall Knot, but make the last tuck up through the centre of the knot, bringing the ends out so that they can be re-laid or whipped, or made into a Sinnet.

When making the knots so far described, you may find it easier to use three strands of different colours, especially on the knots where the lead is doubled. For the knot that I am about to describe, it may save your sanity to do so!

Fig 182   Wall below the Crown.

Fig 181   Double Footrope Knot.

Fig 183   Doubling the Crown.

# Star Knot

This is a mega-knot, complex and somewhat frustrating for the beginner. (My first Star Knot took a whole afternoon to complete, but after about my tenth, I had it down to under the hour! Now I allow about half-an-hour, mainly in the drawing up of the knot after the moves have been completed.) Treat this as your biggest challenge!

It is important to follow the instructions very, very carefully. If necessary, draw out each stage in a way that you can understand.

## Method

I would advise you to start with three strands, and work your way upwards. For me, the five-strand is the most attractive – it seems to look better in odd numbers, and the five has a neat, closed centre. The largest I have completed is a nine strand, but I had to set a three-by-three strand Crown Knot in the centre to fill the hole.

Your strands will need to be about 30cm (12in) long and 2–4mm in diameter. Something fairly stiff like a braided rope is ideal for practising on because it holds the loops well. Seize three lengths together, different colours if possible.

Make an underhand loop in each strand with the previous strand end coming up through, in an anticlockwise direction (see Fig 184). Do not tighten. Make sure the loops do not turn themselves over while you are not looking.

Make a clockwise Crown Knot (see Fig 185). (When I use the terms 'clockwise' and 'anticlockwise', this refers to the direction when you are looking down on the knot from above, unless otherwise stated.) Draw the knot up a little so you can see the two distinct parts, but leave it slack enough for some more tucks.

This is the hardest part. Take one end, loop it around anticlockwise and under itself. It is now running parallel to another strand. Follow this strand down its loop (see Fig 186). Take the next anticlockwise end, pass it under itself *and* the strand that

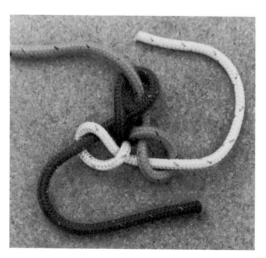

Fig 184   Anticlockwise loops, ends through.

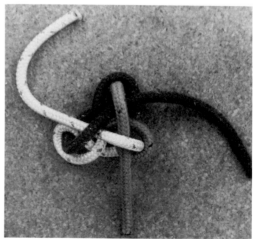

Fig 185   Crown clockwise.

Fig 186   Loop end anticlockwise and under itself.

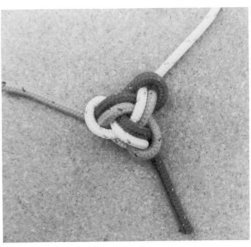

Fig 187   Down through edge loop.

is now alongside it. Follow this strand down through its loop, which has become doubled by the previous move. Take the final end, loop around and under itself and its close friend, and down through its double loop (see Fig 187).

You now have an interlocking trio of double strands showing on the top of the knot, going down through three double loops around the edge. Draw up the knot carefully, taking time over getting the strands in the right place. Do not tighten it completely, you still have work to do!

Look at the knot from underneath. There is a strand coming through each edge loop (see Fig 188). Still looking at the underneath, take an end and lead it to the left (anticlockwise), parallel to the strand already there. Push the end up and into the centre of the knot and out through the top. Do this with the other two strands (see Fig 189).

You now have three strands coming out through the top centre of the knot. If you are working a lanyard, this is the point at

Fig 188   Viewed from underneath – lead strands anticlockwise.

Fig 189    Push ends up through centre.

Fig 190    Lanyard Star Knot.

Fig 191    Terminal Star Knot.

Fig 192    Ends close to stem.

which you lay up the strands and continue on, either whipping the ends or working a sinnet (*see* Fig 190).

Alternatively, you can make it a handsome terminal knot by leading the ends back down through the edge loops again. You will know which end goes through which loop when you look at the knot from the top, but in case you can't, it goes back down through the same loop it went through last time. So, if you use different-coloured strands, push it down alongside its own colour (*see* Fig 191).

The knot is now virtually finished. To be perfect, the strands should be led under the pair of parallel strands on the underside to emerge close against the stem (*see* Fig 192). The ends can then be whipped over the stem, or spliced in on three-strand, or tucked into a Sinnet.

When you have made a few three-stranded Star Knots, progress to a five-stranded one. The technique is exactly the same. Just be careful at the third stage where the end doubles back and under itself. You will notice that it has to go down the next-but-one edge loop. This is just as it was with the three-strand one, but it was not noticeable with only three loops in the game.

When you use more than five strands, the centre will be open, and you will then have to come up with a way to fill it, or cover it. Good luck!

# Sinnets

As a child I happily made yards and yards of tubular knitting, using a cotton reel with four nails hammered into the top.

This was my first Chain Sinnet, though I didn't know it at the time. Single crochet comes under the same heading.

The types of Sinnet I describe here are Crown Sinnets, and they need no tools except your hands. Many are extensions of the Crown Knot made with three of four strands. All are easy to master.

Use small cordage, about 2mm in diameter, and preferably of a natural fibre, which will hold the knots well. Tape the ends to stop them becoming frilly.

## Four-strand Sinnets

1 Bind four cords together with a constrictor, whipping or tape. Working with opposite pairs of cords, tie left-hand Half Knots (left over right) one over the other, making sure that when you put two ends down they are in a natural position between the two ends you pick up. This makes a firm round sinnet (*see* Fig 193).

Fig 193  Four strands, alternate overhand knots.

Fig 194   Crown in one direction.

Fig 195   Alternate Crowns, four strands.

The same technique using right-hand Half Knots will result in a slightly different pattern.

2   Make a succession of Crown Knots, all in the same direction, being sure to draw up the cords evenly (*see* Fig 194).

3   Make a succession of Crown Knots in alternate directions, i.e. one clockwise Crown, one anticlockwise Crown (*see* Fig 195).

## Three-strand Sinnets

These can be made with unlaid three-strand rope, or with three cords bound at one end.

1   Form a series of Crown Knots in the same direction for a small round section (*see* Fig 196).

2   Make alternate left and right crowns (clockwise and anticlockwise) and you have a triangular section sinnet (*see* Fig 197).

Crown Sinnets can be made with any number of strands, but there comes a point where you would need to work them around a core, which can be of rope or something more solid, otherwise the sinnet will collapse inwards.

## Small Projects

Now that we have covered a few decorative knots and sinnets, they can be put together to make small items that can be used as key rings, blind pulls, bell ropes and so on.

The collection in the photograph contains Turks Heads, Star Knots, and

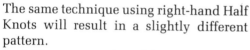

Fig 196 Three-strand Crown Sinnet.

Fig 197 Alternate Crowns, three strands.

different types of Crown Sinnet (*see* Fig 198).

As an example, the one with the split ring consists of three lengths of 2mm cord doubled onto the ring and whipped, making six strands with which to work. A double footrope knot is formed at the top, then the sinnet is made using two lots of three strands alternately crowned clockwise, keeping the strands you have just used on the clockwise side of the ones you are about to pick up. This makes a chunky spiral. The Star Knot at the bottom is made with the six strands, and the ends are stuck through and threaded into the sinnet to finish.

Make up your own patterns by using knots and sinnets in different combinations. Working out the length of cords required can be accomplished by making

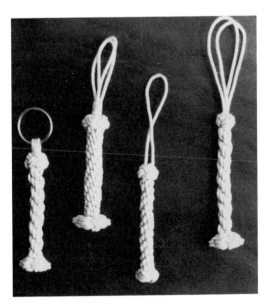

Fig 198 Collection of short Sinnet key fobs.

Fig 199   The Turk's Head Sequence.

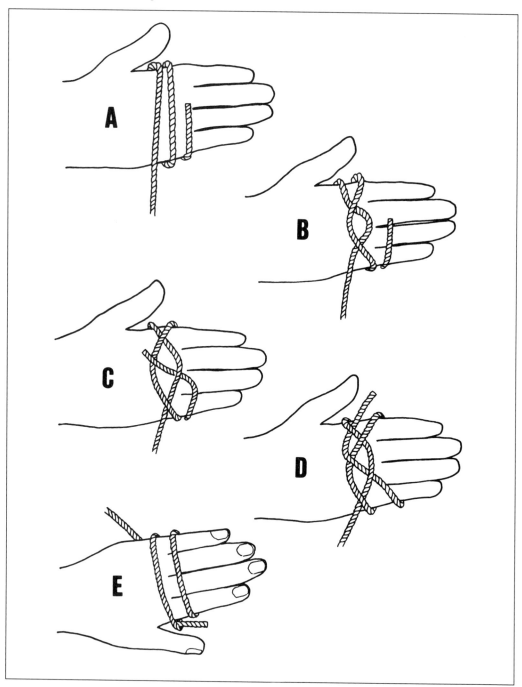

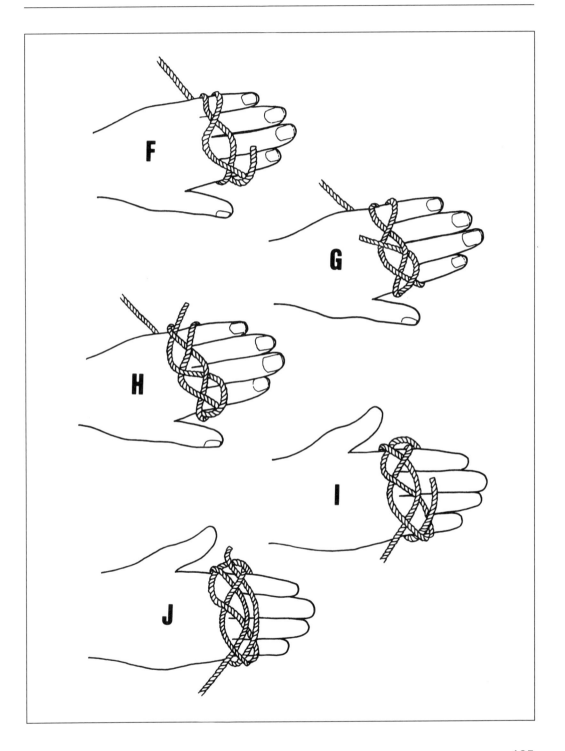

a short length, then undoing it and measuring the used cord. Then simply scale up the measurements to achieve the required length. Long ends can be wound into coils and held with rubber bands.

# The Turk's Head

The Turk's Head could have a chapter all to itself. There are many permutations of bights and leads, widths and lengths. They can be single strand, three strand, multistrand, standing, running, singing and dancing.

Described here is the easiest one (well, *one* of the easiest ones which actually *looks* like a proper Turk's Head) – a single-strand, three-lead, five-bight Turk's Head, and we will make it a three ply (*see* Fig 199).

*Single strand* – this denotes that it is tied with one length of cord.
*Three lead* – denotes that the cord makes three circumnavigations of the article on which you are making it.
*Five bight* – the number of scallops around the edge. (One edge.)
*Three ply* – The end follows around through the turk's head twice more after the initial lead has been completed.

Follow the sequence of diagrams carefully. Wind the cord firmly so that it holds the tucks and loops. A matt surface rope will help with this. The first lead only is shown. Follow around twice more, keeping the end on the correct side all the time, i.e. do not cross the cord to which the end is running parallel.

Use the Turk's Head on oars, boathooks, handrails, in fact anything you want to put a grip on, or purely as a decorative feature. You can cover a multitude of sins, such as

digs in woodwork and raggy ends on coachwhipping. Experiment with more turns and more passes.

# Mats

There is a law which states that the minute you have finished scrubbing your decks, you will be boarded by hoards of jovial revellers shedding inordinate amounts of shingle beach from their boots, later to be ground into the pristine surface which was your deck.

You have only yourself to blame if there isn't a hardwearing but attractive Ocean Plait or two on which they can wipe their wellies.

The Ocean Plait is really just a very large flattened knot, followed around three or four times with one of the ends.

The one shown is an eight-bight mat (*see* Fig 200), eight being the number of 'scallops' around the edge. To make this the size of a useable mat (this one is about 60cm × 35cm/24 × 14in) you will need something in the region of 21m (70ft) of rope of 12–18mm diameter. Sisal has that traditional look, though its tendency towards rotting is a disadvantage. One of the hemp lookalikes would give a reasonably traditional appearance and last longer. A brightly coloured polyester would bring it right up to date. All can be washed to remove the grit.

The method may be unorthodox, but it holds all the bights in place while you complete the first round.

## The Bean-Can Method

You will need eight cans of beans, a flat surface, lots of space and a pair of tweezers if you are using hemp (to extract the

Fig 200   An eight-bight Ocean Plait.

splinters). Write the numbers 1 to 8 on the tops of the cans and arrange them as in the first diagram (*see* Fig 201). Leaving half-a-metre (1½ft) of rope free (you will use it later) feed the bulk of the rope through as follows:

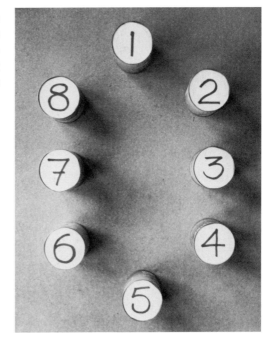

Fig 201   The bean cans, numbered.

in through 5 and 6
out through 2 and 3
in through 1 and 2
out through 7 and 8
in through 6 and 7
thread end under rope and
out through 4 and 5 pulling it all
through (*see* Fig 202)
in through 3 and 4
thread under both ropes then
out through 8 and 1 (*see* Fig 203)
in through 1 and 2
thread under all ropes
out through 6 and 7 still pulling it
all through (*see* Fig 204)

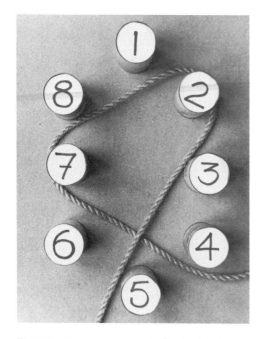

Fig 202   An easy start – note the short end never moves.

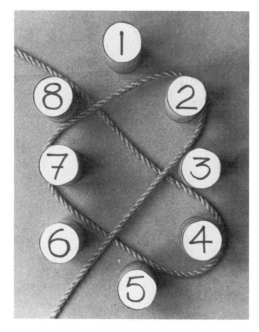

Fig 203   Thread the rope or lift the cans.

Fig 204   End has to be threaded from now on.

Fig 205   You could just lift can 4.

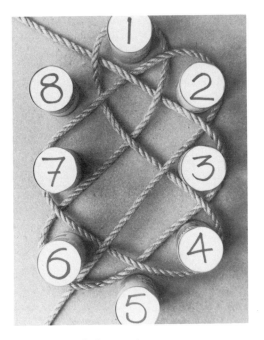

Fig 206    Watch the weaving.

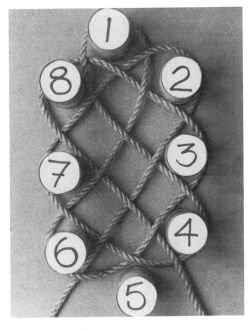

Fig 207    Check yours here against the photograph.

over the free end and
in and through 5 and 6
under both ropes and
out through 3 and 4 (*see* Fig 205)
in through 2 and 3
over, under, over, under,
out through 1 and 8 (*see* Fig 206)
in through 7 and 8
over, under, over, under, over,
out through 4 and 5 (*see* Fig 207)
around 5 and follow end in through
5 and 6 and
go around again, but first check your
pattern against the diagram

as you have now completed one round.
Note the under/over sequences. If it differs
in any way, begin again (*see* Fig 208). At
this point, arrange the cans so that the
bights are evenly spaced, and make the
rope reasonably taut. Follow the first

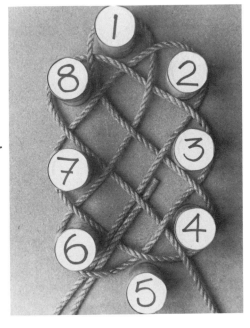

Fig 208    Going around again.

round exactly, making sure all the bights stay flat. You should be able to accommodate at least three rounds, more likely four, and possibly five. For this reason it is always advisable to begin with too much rope. By the way, you should be able to dispense with the bean cans after the first or second round.

As an interesting exercise, try it with some small stuff, using nails in a board. The mat pictured in Fig 209 measures approximately 8 × 5cm (3 × 2in) and is made with 2mm cord.

When the mat is completed, turn it over and rearrange the ends by re-threading so that they rest somewhere towards the centre rather than on the edge, and are not seen from the right side. Finish the ends according to the type of rope used. For safety and wearability the mat should be sewn together on the reverse, a tedious job but well worth the effort. A good addition is a layer of latex solution brushed on, which renders the mat non-slip.

A traditional use for mats is as protection around deck eyes to which blocks are attached. The constant thumping of the blocks on the deck can damage the surface, and a thump mat will also deaden the sound. The mats are usually round, and instructions are given here for a five-bight example. It is, in fact, a flattened-out Turk's Head.

Fig 210 shows the first lead. Follow the lead around twice more and finish the ends. The mat's size can be altered by using a different diameter rope.

This mat can also be made in the hand as in the Turk's Head sequence, and then flattened out.

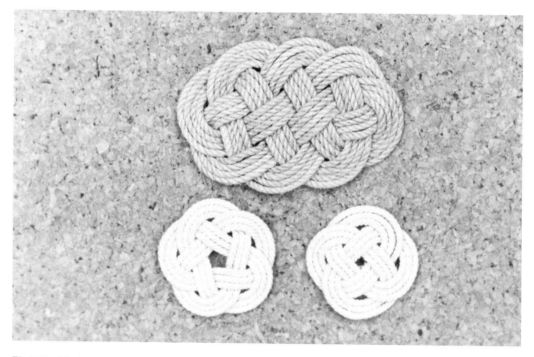

Fig 209   Mini-mats.

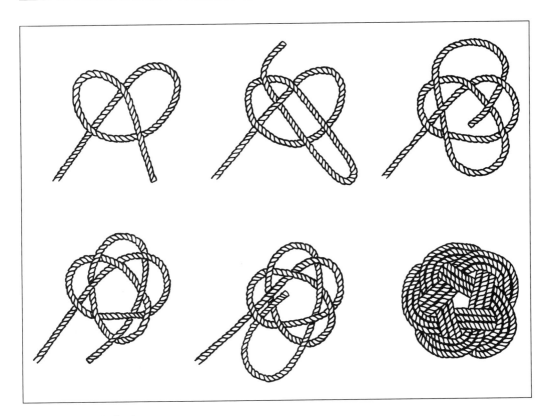

Fig 210   A five-bight thump mat.

## Square Knotting

Hammocks, belts, bags, chair seats, all can be made using a combination of knots which build up to make a 'fabric'.

To the sailor it is square knotting, but it probably originated in Arabia, and enjoyed a popular resurgence in the early 1970s in the worlds of fashion and home décor, in the guise of macramé.

The knots themselves are easy. It is the way in which you combine them that calls for a little ingenuity. I have included some projects for you to try before going on to greater things of your own design.

Estimating lengths of cords is the most difficult part, and you will probably end up with piles of scrap ends – perfect for practising knots!

There is one piece of vital equipment which I find indispensable when square knotting. It consists of a toothbrush handle with a notch in one end and a hole in the other, and was given to me by the seaman to whom I owe my interest in knotting. It is perfectly feasible to make one out of some other material, such as wood, but I have had mine for twenty years and it is still in perfect working order (see Fig 211). It is used in this way – thread a cord through the hole and tie the hook around your waist, over your clothes. The non-working cords are given a turn around the hook and the tension as

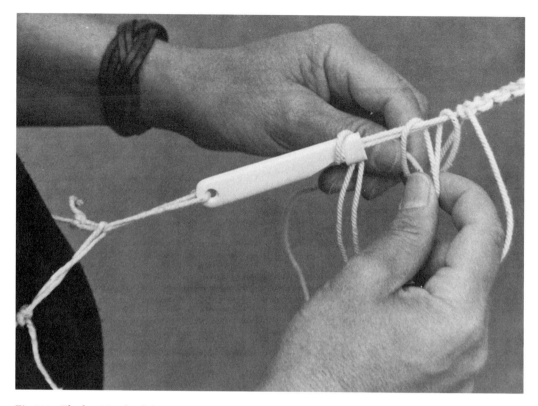

Fig 211   The knotting hook in use.

you lean back locks the ends into place. When you release the tension, the cords are free, and you can pick up the next pair to be worked on.

This may seem unnecessary when working on only four cords as they can be tied directly to a belt, but working on a wider fabric requires the cords to be changed constantly, and the hook saves time and effort. It would be worth making one if you intend to try the projects.

The type of cord you use depends entirely on what you are making – sisal for plant hangers, silk for bikinis – but parcel string is fine for practising.

Square knotting begins with a foundation cord, onto which are hitched any number of vertical working cords, depending upon the width of fabric required. To start with, we will practise on just four cords.

There are only two basic knots to learn, the Square Knot and the Half Hitch. You are already familiar with the latter, so we will get straight into the Square Knot (sometimes called the Flat Knot, but not by me).

## Method

To make a short decorative cord, cut two pieces of string about 4m (13ft) long. Cut a shorter piece to use as a foundation cord. About 50cm (20in) should suffice, and it needs to be attached to something solid

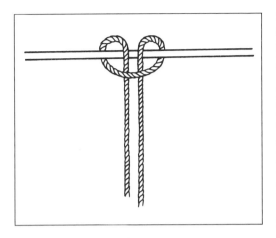

Fig 212  The Cow Hitch.

like a door handle or your old faithful table leg.

The customary way of attaching a working cord to the foundation cord is by way of a Cow Hitch. This is what you get when you tie two Half Hitches in opposite directions (*see* Fig 212). You can also make it by doubling the cord into a loop, and using your thumb and forefinger protruding downwards through the loop to hook the ends through.

So, using Cow Hitches, attach one of the long pieces to the short so that one end hangs down about 1m (3ft). Do the same with the other piece, with the two shorter ends being in the middle between the two longer ends. This is because the middle two will act as a core around which the longer ends will be knotted.

Loop the foundation cord onto your immovable object, and hitch the two centre cords around your waist hook, or tie to your belt.

The Square Knot is in fact a Reef Knot formed around a central core. It can be performed in two movements, which are known as Half Knots, which can also be used singly.

To make one Half Knot, take the end of the *left cord across the front* of the centre core, take the end of the *right cord across*

Fig 213  Left in front, right behind.

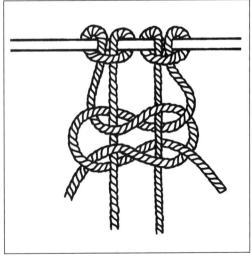

Fig 214  Cross right cord in front, left cord behind; two Half Knots make a square knot.

Fig 215    Make a loop across the front.

Fig 216    Finger and thumb through loop.

Fig 217    Grasp neck of loop.

Fig 218    Pull it back through.

Fig 219    Pass working cord down through loop.

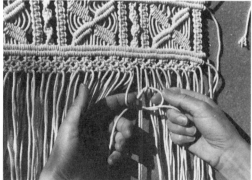

Fig 220    Rearrange the loops.

114

Fig 221    Tighten first Half Knot.

Fig 222    Tighten second Half Knot.

*the back.* Put the ends through the loops so formed and draw up the knot to the top of the cords (*see* Fig 213). This is one Half Knot. Repeat the sequence a few times and you will see how it builds into a spiral pattern, called a Bannister Bar (*see* Fig 223).

Now make a Half Knot in the other direction, crossing the *right cord in front* and the *left cord behind* (*see* Fig 214). Make several and you have a Bannister Bar spiralling in the opposite direction.

You can deduce from this that if you alternate the Half Knots, the bar will not spiral but will stay flat, so you have discovered that the Square Knot consists of two alternating Half Knots.

There is a way of tying the Square Knot in one movement, i.e. both left- and right-hand Half Knots together to make a complete Square Knot. It is complicated to describe, but so much quicker to make when you have acquired the knack.

Tension the two central core cords as before. Using the left-hand working cord, make a loop across the front of the core (*see* Fig 215). With your right thumb and forefinger, reach down through the loop, grasp the neck of the loop from under-

neath and pull it back through (*see* Figs 216, 217 and 218), giving you a sort of 'cow-hitch loop' around the core. Take the right-hand working cord and pass it through the space made by your thumb and forefinger, towards you, i.e. from top to bottom (*see* Fig 219). What you have now looks like an almighty mess, but if you take the two loose working ends in your little fingers, and the two upper ends in your thumbs and forefingers, a little rearranging will give you a Square Knot which can be pulled tight in two movements (*see* Figs 220, 221 and 222). It takes practice, and you may prefer to use different fingers, but when mastered, this method is twice as fast as the two Half Knots method.

Make a row of several Square Knots, using first the alternating Half-Knot method, then the 'all-in-one' method. The tension will become more even as you become more proficient. The vertical row of square knots is called a Solomon Bar (*see* Fig 223).

The Half Hitch is used in the normal way, using the outer cords alternately to make hitches around the central core. Try making a row of alternate hitches, then

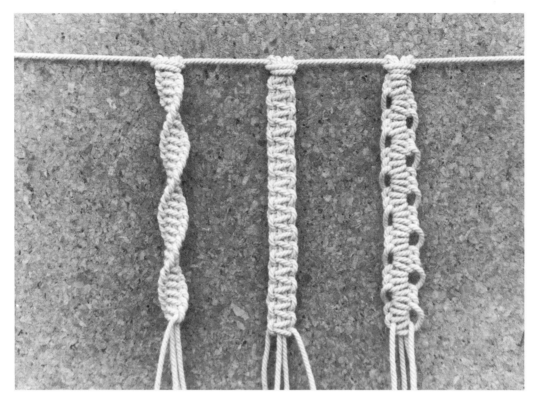

Fig 223    Left to right: Bannister Bar; Solomon Bar; Genoese Bar.

increase the number in each movement, i.e. make three hitches left, three hitches right, for about 10cm (4in). This gives a looped edge pattern called a Genoese Bar, but do not pull the loops too tightly when beginning each group of hitches (*see* Fig 223).

With just these basic knots you can make any number of decorative cords, inserting Wall and Crown Knots, Matthew Walkers and the like to denote a transition. For something a little more substantial, like a hammock, the technique is the same but the number of cords is increased and they are alternated during the knotting, becoming working cords on some rows and core cords on others. To demonstrate

this we should go straight into the projects, otherwise you will be snowed under by scraps of useless knotted flotsam.

# Project 1 Bookmark

Cut 6 cords 1m (3ft) long.

Double them onto a short horizontal cord of about 40cm (16in) making them all approximately the same length.

Using the first four cords, make five Square Knots. Repeat with the next four cords, then the next, giving you three Solomon Bars of five Square Knots (*see* Fig 224).

116

Fig 224   Three Solomon Bars.

Fig 225   Use core cords as working cords.

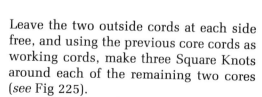

Leave the two outside cords at each side free, and using the previous core cords as working cords, make three Square Knots around each of the remaining two cores (*see* Fig 225).

Now go back to the original pattern and make another three bars of five, then another two bars of three, so you have three bars at the top, then two, then three, then two (*see* Fig 226).

Now, make one Square Knot with the first four cords, one with the second four, and one with the remaining four.

Next row, leave outside two at each side. Make a Square Knot with each of the remaining groups (two in all).

Next row, make one Square Knot with the middle four.

You now have knots coming to a 'V' shape at the bottom (*see* Fig 227).

Fig 226   Three, two, three, two.

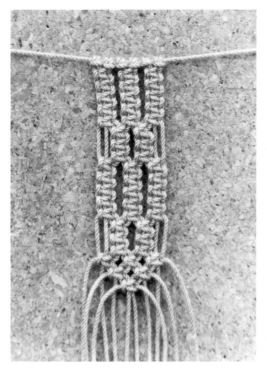

Fig 227   Knots coming to a 'V'.

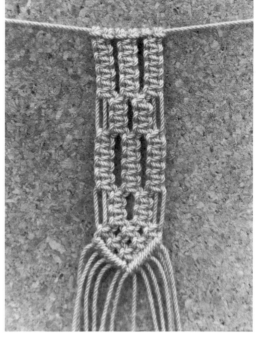

Fig 228   First row of cording.

Another technique needs to be introduced here, called Cording. It consists of Half Hitches around a *leader cord*.

In this case the leader cords are those on the outer edges of your bookmark. Starting on the left, take the outside cord across to the centre but at a downward angle of about 45 degrees, following the square knots just completed. Starting from the outside and working inwards, make two Half Hitches around the leader cord with each cord in turn until you reach the centre. Repeat this on the right-hand side (*see* Fig 228). This gives you one row of cording, but it is preferable to repeat the sequence so you have two close rows of cording to finish. The last thing to do is trim the ends to about 5cm (2in) and tease

out the strands to give a fringe. The foundation cord can be knotted on either side and trimmed, tied into a loop if you want to use it as a hanging, or knotted through a paper clip to attach it to a book spine (*see* Fig 229).

From the knots in this simple piece, you can make far more complicated items. Something of use on a boat is a sailor's stowaway, a pocket to hang beside a bunk (*see* Fig 230). It is quite a large project, but you do not have to complete it in one sitting. I have given outline instructions only – it is not necessary to detail every knot. Work the horizontal cording using separate leaders, which are sewn into the back of the work when it is completed. It does not matter in which direction you

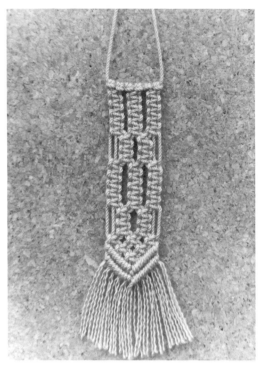

Fig 229   Finished bookmark.

Fig 230   A stowaway.

make the Half Hitches on the cording, provided you are consistent.

You can change the dimensions if you wish by adding or subtracting cords, and making more rows of knotting, but remember to allow for this when measuring the cords.

The foundation cord needs to be under a fair amount of tension. One way of achieving this is to work the piece on a board, enabling you to fix the ends to nails or pins in the board. You can also pin the sides as you work, avoiding any tendency toward 'pulled in' edges.

The finished size will also be affected if you use cord of a different diameter, which can be useful if you want a matching set in different sizes.

## Project 2 Stowaway

You will need about 125m (410ft) of cord about 2mm thick. This will make a pocket about 30cm (12in) wide. It will need to be mounted on a piece of canvas, unless you are aiming to tack it straight to the bulkhead. You will also need a pack of sticking plasters – for the blisters.

Cut a foundation cord of about 60cm (2ft) and pin it to a board.

Alternatively, cut it long enough to tie between two solid points if you are not using a board.

Cut eight lengths of 60cm (2ft) to use as leaders for the horizontal cording.

Cut 36 lengths of 3m (9ft) for the working cords.

119

Fig 231   Horizontal cording underway.

Fig 232   Watch the centre of the diagonal.

Fig 233   The first leader is hitched around the second leader.

Fig 234   Hitch the left leader on to the right leader.

Double the working cords onto the foundation cord with Cow Hitches.

Attach one of the cut leaders to your board. Make a row of cording close up to the hitches.

Repeat using another leader (*see* Fig 231). Working in groups of four cords, make a row of square knots across the work.

Make another row, using alternate groups of four.

Repeat these two rows until you have seven rows of Square Knots altogether.

Make two rows of cording using two of the cut leaders.

Now follow the pattern for the centre panel, using four cords for each Solomon Bar, three for the Bannister Bars (only one core cord) and 14 cords for the diagonal-cording sections. Follow the diagrams carefully (*see* Figs 232–236).

You are more than half-way now!

Fig 235  Carry on with the same leader.

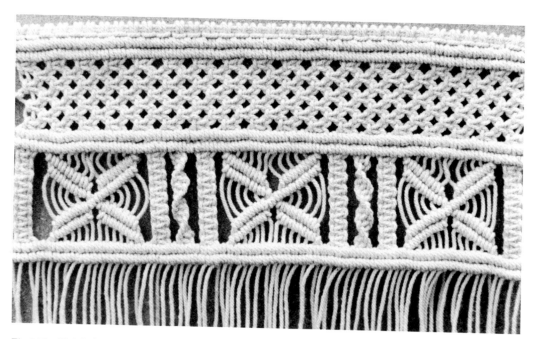

Fig 236  Finish the panel with two rows of horizontal cording.

Make two more horizontal rows of cording, then on to the alternate Square Knots, seven rows.

The next two rows of cording are the last, but don't cheer yet, there is still some finishing off to do.

Cut off the cords at about 7cm (3in) and fringe the ends.

This is the actual knotting finished, but there is some tidying to be done. The leader cords can be knotted and left hanging, or sewn into the back of the work. The pocket now needs to be sewn onto a piece of canvas which is large enough to provide a surround of several centimetres.

Pockets look good in pairs, one above the other, so you could make two and mount them on one large piece of canvas.

Make a large hem at the top through which to feed a dowel rod. This can be hooked over two screw eyes on the wall or bulkhead. Alternatively, you could set some brass cringles into the top, using one of the readily available kits, and again, mount it on screw eyes.

Originally, the stowaway would have been made in canvas, with parts of the fabric deliberately frayed by removing the weft threads. The knotting was then carried out on the warp. The version above is a modern interpretation.

**SUMMARY**

- Natural fibre makes for better fancy work.

- Begin with a small project and work towards the more complex.

- Use your imagination!

# 13

# ROPES FOR CLASSIC BOATS

Throughout this book I have tended to gravitate towards the modern yacht with regard to fibres, but with the recent upsurge of interest in preserving our sailing heritage, indeed even reproducing it in the original materials, there has been an increase in the demand for ropes and chandlery in keeping with the classic designs.

Brightly coloured polyester braids do not sit well against tan sails and varnished bowsprits. Hemp and manila, the traditional choice, are still used by the purist, but the disadvantages are many – low resistance to weathering, susceptibility to rotting, heavy weight, lack of strength, though an interesting point is that both are stronger when wet.

Another problem is availability. These natural fibres are not easy to find in yacht chandlers, but fortunately there are still specialist suppliers.

For halyards, all these problems can be largely overcome by the use of imitations. These are three-strand polypropylene ropes, brown in colour, and looking remarkably like the real thing, complete with hairs!

There are many to choose from, all with similar properties. Most are hemp look-alikes, light brown with a soft, hairy finish, like 'Synthemp' from Liros, 'Hardyhemp' from Marlow and 'Spuntex' from Roblon. There is also a darker brown manila lookalike from Roblon called 'Spunflex', with a shiny finish which weathers to an interesting dull 'used' look. It is stronger than the softer ones, and is used extensively on square riggers.

Being synthetic, these ropes have a much greater breaking strength than the natural fibres (approximately double) but they also suffer the disadvantages of any polypropylene rope – poor resistance to abrasion and high sensitivity to ultra violet light, though this is in comparison to polyesters. Matched against the natural fibres they imitate, the qualities they display are very similar, with extra points for the synthetics' strength advantage.

The difficulty arises when it comes to choosing sheets. I can remember cotton sheets on sailing boats (I was very young!). They were soft on the hands, and did not seem to kink unduly. They were always 'inch and a quarter', and that referred to the circumference, the way in which rope was universally measured. Cotton is still available from specialist suppliers, but why can't the big manufacturers come up with a dull brown braided polyester which would not look out of place in a traditional setting? They seem to manage every other colour you could possibly want.

Until then, the darker colours would seem the most appropriate. Each manufacturer has its own particular shades, but plain black is available from Marlow, also from Liros (with a small fleck) and dark green and a darkish red from Roblon and Liros. I have tried home dying, but polyester is notoriously difficult to dye successfully. The best result was achieved by using a black multi-purpose dye from Dylon International on a red polyester braid (anybody's), giving an agreeably subdued reddish-brown hue, which has a certain affinity with the tan synthetic canvas substitute used extensively for classic boat sails.

If you think this is going too far for the sake of aesthetics, then lobby the manufacturers to do something for the classics enthusiast.

The natural fibres show their superiority in any knotting situation of a decorative nature. The fact that they are non-slip means they hold a knot extremely well, which can make splicing and sinnet work a real pleasure, especially after grappling with a slippery synthetic.

For small fancy work, cotton and flax are suitable. Mats look well in sisal and manila, though a synthetic substitute can be used. Traditional boats lend themselves beautifully to fancy work, and you can amuse yourselves for hours making bell ropes, thump mats, strops and all manner of decoration.

Take the Turk's Head. It can be put on oars, guardrails, fishing rods, paddles, poles, tools, wrists, in fact anything that is vaguely round sectioned and keeps still for ten minutes.

Convenient finger pulls can be made to adorn snapshackles by attaching short sinnets.

Anti-chafe gear can be far more attractive on board a traditional boat than on a plastic racer. Bits of plastic tube may be perfectly serviceable, but a strip of chromed leather sewn around your mooring ropes has that certain something extra. Use stout twine and make the leather slightly smaller than the rope circumference as it will stretch when you pull tight the stitches. This gives it a good tight fit and it will mould onto the rope when it gets wet.

And what about baggywrinkle? There's no better way of protecting your sails than to have bunches of yarns like imitation hedgehogs climbing up the rigging. It is not difficult to make and is a good way of using up any old ends. Chop them into 20cm (8in) lengths and separate them into yarns. Hitch them onto a pair of parallel cords, using a wooden spacer with notches in to assist in keeping the cords apart. Pack the thrums down tightly. When you have completed the required length, it is wound around the shrouds and spreaders, and seized on at the ends.

Shrouds can also be covered in French Whipping, or sinnets of Half Knots and Crown Knots. Put on a Turk's Head at the point where they are seized onto the rigging.

You can improve your classic standing in harbour by making some real fenders, instead of having to sport those blue and white inflated sausages. Make them from thick coir if you can get hold of it. (You may even find something suitable washed up on the shore.) A firm fender can be made by doubling the rope and making a Crown Sinnet with all six strands. Make it the length you require, then finish with a Crown, then a Wall, both doubled.

Larger fenders can be made in the same way but with a piece of plastic or rubber hose in the centre of the Sinnet as a core around which to knot.

Even larger fenders can be made by disguising the ubiquitous sausage with Half Hitching. Start by making a loop in the rope and put Half Hitches around it. The idea is to make rows of Half Hitches into the preceding rows, gradually covering the fender. You can increase and decrease to take account of the shape by hitching twice into a space, and missing a space, respectively. It is time consuming and rope consuming, but it does give you a good resilient fender.

There are other decorative touches you can add, pertinent to craft of a traditional nature, like fancy handles, drawer pulls, chest beckets and picture frames, which warrant a book all to themselves.

### SUMMARY

- On a classic boat, you may have to compromise on fibre in order to obtain sufficient strength.

- Use decorative knots to add traditional touches like bell ropes, mats and real fenders.

# GLOSSARY

**Aramid**  A generic term for a particularly strong polymer fibre used in modern ropes.

**Backsplice**  A splice at the end of a rope to stop it unlaying.
**Baggywrinkle**  Anti-chafe gear fixed to the rigging, made from short ends of rope or rags.
**Becket**  A closed eye or hook. Also the rope handle of a sea chest.
**Bend**  Denotes a knot used to join two ropes together.
**Bight**  The part of a rope between the ends, when curved into a loop.
**Bitter end**  The end of a rope.
**Block**  A pulley through which rope is rove.
**Bollard**  A mooring post.
**Breaking strength**  The load required to cause a rope to break under tension.
**Breast ropes**  Short mooring ropes running perpendicular to the centreline, to assist in keeping in the ends of the boat.

**Capsize**  Where a knot changes its form under tension, giving it the potential to come adrift.
**Chafe**  Abrasion and fraying of a rope.
**Cleat**  Deck or mast fitting with two horns on which to secure ropes.
**Codline**  Small three-stranded hemp rope.
**Cross whipping**  A way of finishing a splice by whipping together half of each strand to the adjacent half.

**Dogging**  Making several turns around a rope with a smaller rope, with the lay. A way of attaching blocks to stays.

**End**  The end of the rope.
**End for end**  Turning ropes up the other way to even the wear.
**Eye splice**  Making a permanent loop in the end of a rope by weaving the end into the body of the rope.

**Fid**  A tapered tool used in splicing.
**Frapping turns**  Rounds of twine at right angles to the whipping or seizing on which they are made, to tighten the initial layer of turns.
**Full tuck**  A round of tucks in splicing.

**Halyards**  Ropes used to hoist sails.
**Hank**  A coil of rope, usually with crossing turns, ready to hang up.
**Hemp**  A natural fibre used in rope-making.
**Hitch**  Denotes a knot used to make a rope fast to a fixed point.

**Kevlar**  A registered trade name for an Aramid fibre.
**Knot**  Denotes a stopper on the end of a rope, but the term is loosely used for any hitch, knot or bend.

**Lanyard**  Short length of cord often attached to knives, tools, buckets, etc.
**Lay**  The manufactured twist in a rope.

**Line stopper** A mechanical device for holding a rope in position. Quick to release.
**Loop** Another term for bight.

**Marline spike** A tool used to part strands of rope or wire.

**Palm, sailmaker's** A piece of shaped leather worn on the hand, with a metal dimpled insert with which to push sail needles through rope and fabric.

**Reeve** To thread a rope, through a block for example.
**Riders, riding turns** What you get on a winch when you don't concentrate. The loose bottom turns ride up over the upper turns and get trapped, rendering the winch useless until they can be cleared. In whipping and seizing, the second layer of turns.
**Rope** General term for cordage.
**Round turn** A 540-degree wrap of the rope – a turn and a half.
**Running rigging** Halyards, running backstays, topping lifts, spinnaker pole uphauls. Any rigging which is rove through blocks.

**Seizing** Joining two ropes or two parts of a rope together by binding with twine.
**Sheave** A pulley wheel in a block which bears the rope.
**Sheets** The trimming ropes attached to sails.

**Sinnet** A decorative braid of cord.
**Soft eye** One without a thimble inserted.
**Spring** A mooring rope running diagonally, from bow and stern.
**Standing part** The non-working part of a rope.
**Standing rigging** Shrouds and stays.
**Stopper** Strictly speaking, a terminal knot with the end coming out of the top, relaid and whipped. Also used to denote a knot on a rope to stop it unreeving, such as a Figure of Eight.
**Strands** Yarns twisted together during rope manufacture.

**Thimble** A metal or nylon insert often spliced into an eye to protect the rope against chafing from shackles and other hardware.
**Thrum** A short length of rope, yarn, etc.
**Tuck** A movement during splicing where one strand is led under another.
**Turn** A 360-degree wrap of the rope.

**Unlay** To untwist or take apart a rope.

**Warp** Another term used for rope, especially in a mooring situation.
**Whipping** Wrapping the end of a rope with twine to prevent fraying.
**Working part** The part of a rope which is being used to make a knot.

**Yarn** Fibres twisted together.

# INDEX